Earth's Incredible Habitats
Desert

Written by
Anita Ganeri

Illustrated by
Federico Epis

Written by Anita Ganeri
Illustrated by Federico Epis

Senior editor Radhika Haswani
Project editor Srijani Ganguly
Project art editor Bhagyashree Nayak
Art editors Nishtha Gupta, Debjyoti Mukherjee
Assistant art editor Tanya Varkey P
Pre-production designer Dheeraj Singh
Pre-production image editor Mohd Rizwan
Senior picture researcher Sakshi Saluja
Jacket designer Rashika Kachroo
Jacket illustrator Joe Stansbury
Jacket coordinator Elin Woosnam
Managing editor Roohi Sehgal
Managing art editors Diane Peyton Jones, Ivy Sengupta
Production editor Dragana Puvacic
Senior production controller Leanne Burke
Creative head Malavika Talukder
Publisher James Mitchem
Art director Mabel Chan

Consultant Douglas Palmer

First published in Great Britain in 2025 by
Dorling Kindersley Limited
20 Vauxhall Bridge Road,
London SW1V 2SA

The authorised representative in the EEA is
Dorling Kindersley Verlag GmbH. Arnulfstr. 124,
80636 Munich, Germany

Copyright © 2025 Dorling Kindersley Limited
A Penguin Random House Company
10 9 8 7 6 5 4 3 2 1
001–351125–Jan/2026

All rights reserved.
No part of this publication may be reproduced, stored in or introduced into a retrieval system, or transmitted, in any form, or by any means (electronic, mechanical, photocopying, recording, or otherwise), without the prior written permission of the copyright owner. No part of this publication may be used or reproduced in any manner for the purpose of training artificial intelligence technologies or systems. In accordance with Article 4(3) of the DSM Directive 2019/790, DK expressly reserves this work from the text and data mining exception.

A CIP catalogue record for this book
is available from the British Library.
ISBN: 978-0-2417-5982-0

Printed and bound in China

www.dk.com

MIX
Paper | Supporting responsible forestry
FSC™ C018179

This book was made with Forest Stewardship Council™ certified paper – one small step in DK's commitment to a sustainable future.
Learn more at www.dk.com/uk/information/sustainability

Contents

- 4 North America
- 6 South America
- 8 Africa
- 10 Asia
- 12 Oceania
- 14 Antarctica

- 16 What is a desert?
- 18 Different deserts
- 20 Deserts of the world
- 22 Sands and landforms
- 24 Threats

HOT AND DRY DESERTS

- 28 Sahara Desert
- 30 Geography of the Sahara Desert
- 32 Animals of the Sahara Desert
- 34 Dromedary camel
- 36 Plants of the Sahara Desert
- 38 Desert duststorm
- 40 Mojave Desert
- 42 Geography of the Mojave Desert
- 44 Animals of the Mojave Desert

46 Plants of the Mojave Desert
48 Joshua tree
50 Death Valley
52 Thar Desert
54 Geography of the Thar Desert
56 Animals of the Thar Desert
58 Great Indian bustard
60 Plants of the Thar Desert
62 Lake Sambhar
64 Arabian Desert
66 Geography of the Arabian Desert
68 Animals of the Arabian Desert
70 Arabian oryx
72 Plants of the Arabian Desert
74 Rub' al-Khali
76 Great Victoria Desert
78 Geography of the Great Victoria Desert
80 Animals of the Great Victoria Desert
82 Desert devil
84 Plants of the Great Victoria Desert
86 Nullarbor Plain

COASTAL DESERTS
90 Atacama Desert
92 Geography of the Atacama Desert
94 Animals of the Atacama Desert
96 Andean flamingo
98 Plants of the Atacama Desert
100 Valley of the Moon
102 Namib Desert
104 Geography of the Namib Desert
106 Animals of the Namib Desert
108 Plants of the Namib Desert
110 Tumboa
112 Skeleton Coast

COLD WINTER DESERTS
116 Gobi Desert
118 Geography of the Gobi Desert
120 Animals of the Gobi Desert
122 Pallas's cat
124 Plants of the Gobi Desert
126 Nemegt Basin

128 Great Basin Desert
130 Geography of the Great Basin Desert
132 Animals of the Great Basin Desert
134 Spadefoot toad
136 Plants of the Great Basin Desert
138 Cathedral Gorge

POLAR DESERTS
142 Antarctica
144 Geography of Antarctica
146 Animals of Antarctica
148 Emperor penguin
150 Plants of Antarctica
152 Icebergs

154 Glossary
156 Index
158 Acknowledgements

North America

North America is home to four mighty deserts – the Great Basin, Mojave, Sonoran, and Chihuahuan. Among them, the Sonoran bursts with the richest variety of plants. Giant saguaro, USA's largest cacti, tower over this desert – the only place where they grow naturally. These deserts extend across the western and southwestern USA and northern Mexico, sharing interconnected landscapes and many common features.

South America

This imposing, snow-capped volcano is one of several that rise thousands of metres above the Atacama Desert in Chile. The Atacama is probably the most famous desert in South America, but it is not the only one. Deserts can also be found in Peru, Columbia, and Bolivia, while in Argentina, the vast Patagonian Desert is sandwiched between the Andes Mountains and the Atlantic Ocean.

Africa

In Africa's sprawling Kalahari Desert, ostriches — the world's largest birds — thrive against the odds. They rely on their strength and speed to outrun fierce sandstorms, which often sweep through the area. Apart from the Kalahari, nearly 40 per cent of the African continent is covered by deserts. These include the Namib and Karoo in the south, the Danakil in the east, and, in the north, the enormous Sahara — the largest hot desert on Earth.

Asia

The Taklamakan Desert in China has rolling sand dunes, rocky plains, and snow-capped mountains on three sides. This desolate place lives up to its name, which means "the place of no return" in the local language. To the east of the Taklamakan lies the Gobi, Asia's second-largest desert. It is beaten in size only by the Arabian, which covers most of the Arabian Peninsula.

Oceania

All of the great deserts of Oceania are found in Australia, including the Great Victoria and Great Sandy Desert. Around one-fifth of the country is classed as desert, or the "outback", and is renowned for its bright red sands. Rising from the heart of this "Red Centre" is Uluru, a massive sandstone rock or monolith. Dating back hundreds of millions of years, it is a sacred site for the First Australians.

Antarctica

Despite being mostly covered in ice, the continent of Antarctica counts as a desert because it is so dry. In fact, it is the driest place on Earth, as well as the coldest and windiest. Part of this vast polar desert, the McMurdo Dry Valleys are rare, ice-free regions. Among the most extreme environments on the planet, some places here have not seen rain for millions of years.

DESERT

What is a desert?

When you think of a desert, you probably imagine sweltering heat and expansive dunes. But some deserts are rocky, stony, or even covered in ice. Their climates vary, too – from unbearably hot summers to freezing winters, either seasonally or all year. Most experts define a desert as a place that receives less than 250 mm (10 in) of rain a year, with little water for people and wildlife.

Desert habitats

At first sight, deserts might seem empty and lifeless, but an astonishing range of plants and animals live there. They occupy many different habitats – in the sand, underground, on rocky slopes, among plant stems and leaves, and near rare, often temporary, pools of water.

Birds of prey soar above the desert, looking for their next meal.

Coyotes are among many mammals that live in deserts.

Desert species

The scorching, bone-dry conditions make deserts hostile habitats for plants and animals. Desert species have adapted to the lack of water, heat, and other challenges by changing their lifestyles and developing a range of special features.

Desert food web

In any habitat, plants and animals are linked by what they eat. The desert food web begins with plants, including grasses and cacti. These are eaten by herbivores, such as small mammals and lizards. In turn, they provide food for carnivores, such as foxes and birds of prey.

Staying cool

Like many other desert animals, fennec foxes shelter in the day and come out to look for food at night when it is cooler. They also give off heat through their large ears, to stop them from overheating.

Saving water

Desert plants, such as cacti and succulents, have various ways of surviving. Instead of leaves, they have long, thin spines to reduce the amount of water loss. These plants can also store water in their thick, fleshy stems.

Tough terrain

Getting around different types of desert terrain can be quite problematic. Some animals, such as the sidewinder, find interesting ways to do so. The snake moves its body in a series of "S-shaped" curves to avoid getting burned by the hot sand.

DESERT

Desert types

There are hot and dry (or sub-tropical) deserts like the Sahara, coastal deserts such as the Atacama, cold winter or semi-arid deserts like the Gobi, and polar deserts such as Antarctica. Throughout this book, we will look at deserts from each of the four main types.

Hot and dry

Coastal

Cold winter

Polar

Different deserts

Although all deserts are dry, they vary in many ways. Deserts can be grouped by location – including inland, along coasts, on the sheltered sides of mountains, or near the poles. However, climate and physical features are also important and help distinguish one type from another.

As the air rises, it cools and forms clouds that bring rain.

Dry air flows over the top and down the other side.

Moist air from the sea is forced to rise.

Sea

Windward side

Mountains

Leeward side

Desert

In the shadows

Some deserts form on the leeward, or sheltered, side of tall mountain ranges. Moist air from the windward side is blocked by the mountains, so little or no rain reaches the other side. This dry leeward area is said to have a "rain shadow".

DIFFERENT DESERTS

Deserts in space

Apart from Earth, Mars is also famous for its deserts. Its surface is covered in dunes formed from sand, dust, and rock. Some of the dunes have a similar shape to those found on Earth. Others, such as hexagonal dunes, are unique to Mars.

Mountain desert

A rare type of desert, called a montane desert, is found high up in some mountains. These deserts, like the one in the Kunlun Mountains, are extremely dry because they lie far away from any sources of moisture. Most are also very cold, though daytime temperatures can be scorching.

Arctic
The northernmost parts of the Arctic region count as desert because they are so dry.

Great Basin

Colorado Plateau
This arid land is dotted with plateaus and canyons, including the famous Grand Canyon.

Mojave Desert

Chihuahuan Desert
This desert is largely sandwiched between the two Sierra Madre mountain ranges of Mexico.

Sonoran Desert
Situated to the south of the Mojave, this desert lies mostly in Arizona, USA.

Sahara Desert

Atacama Desert

Patagonian Desert
In the rain shadow of the Andes Mountains, this desert is cold, dry, and very windy.

Deserts of the world

You may have heard of some popular deserts, such as the Sahara, but how many of the world's other deserts do you know? This map shows the deserts featured in this book, with a few others for you to explore. Deserts are found all over the world, in every continent apart from Europe. Now, it is over to you to decide where you want to begin your tour.

DESERT

Types of sand dune

Sand dunes form when the wind blows loose sand into piles. Dunes come in different sizes and shapes, depending on which direction the wind is blowing from. Over time, dunes slowly shift as sand is blown up the windward side and slides down the leeward slope.

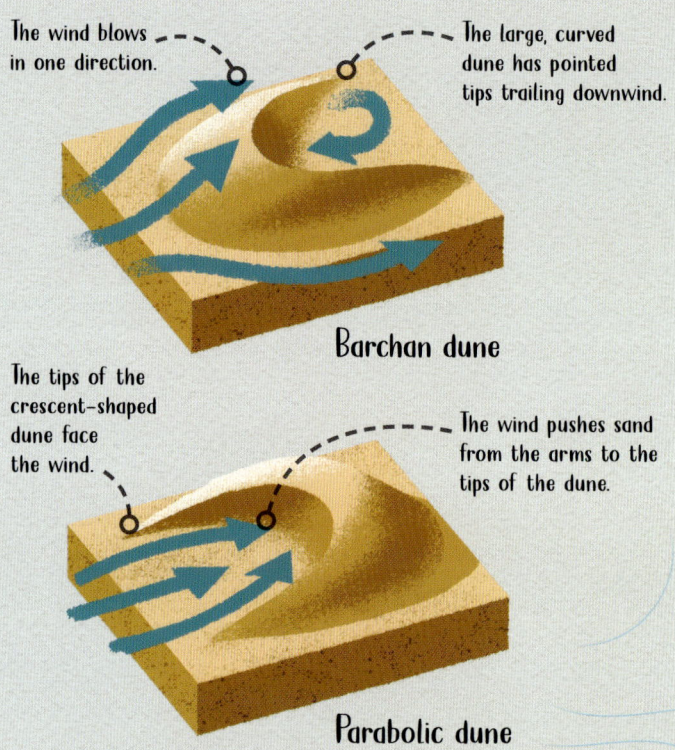

The wind blows in one direction.
The large, curved dune has pointed tips trailing downwind.

Barchan dune

The tips of the crescent-shaped dune face the wind.
The wind pushes sand from the arms to the tips of the dune.

Parabolic dune

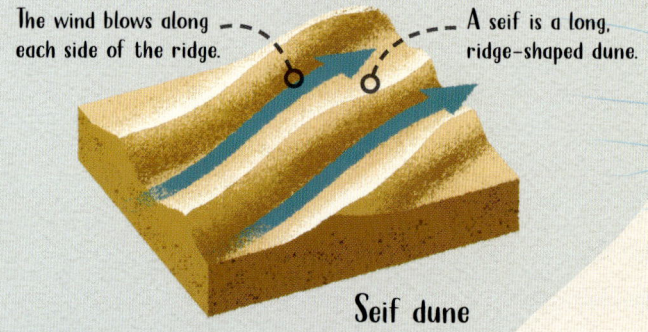

The wind blows along each side of the ridge.
A seif is a long, ridge-shaped dune.

Seif dune

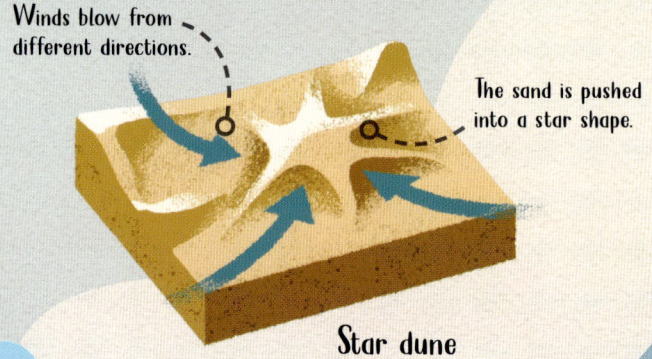

Winds blow from different directions.
The sand is pushed into a star shape.

Star dune

Sands and landforms

The landscape of a desert is shaped by erosion – a slow process where wind, water, or weather break down rock over time. Erosion can happen in many ways. Desert winds blast sand against rock surfaces. Sudden floods sweep sand and gravel, dumping them on the desert floor. The moisture heats up and expands in the day, then freezes at night, causing the rocks to break apart.

Sand grains can be big and coarse or small and fine.

Sand

The sand that covers some deserts is made up of tiny fragments of rocks and minerals, broken down by erosion. Some sand is formed in the desert itself, but much of it is transported from other places by wind or water.

Mesas and buttes

Mushroom rocks

Yardangs

Gibber plains

Desert features

As the wind and water erode, or wear away at the desert, they carve out spectacular features and shapes into the rocks. These striking landforms include mesas and buttes, mushroom rocks, yardangs, and gibber plains, also known as desert pavements.

Moving sand

Grains of sand are picked up by wind and carried across the desert in different ways. Some are blown high into the air, while others bounce or skip along the ground. The rest roll across the surface, colliding with other grains in their path and pushing them along, too.

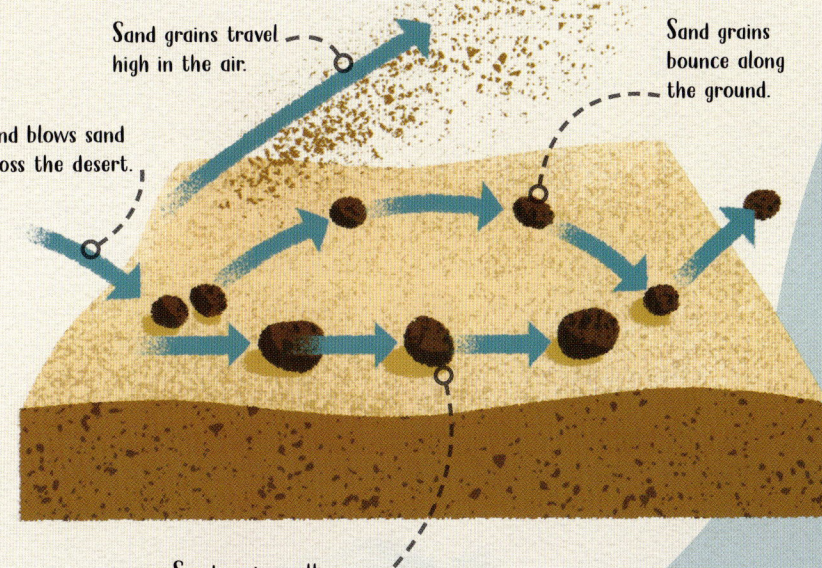

Sand grains travel high in the air.

Sand grains bounce along the ground.

Wind blows sand across the desert.

Sand grains roll across the ground.

DESERT

Threats

Around the world, deserts and their unique wildlife are increasingly at risk. Global warming, soil erosion, and sudden, intense floods (or flash flooding) all pose serious threats. Desert habitats are fragile, with plants, animals, and their environments intricately connected. Even small changes in temperature or rainfall can disrupt the delicate balance. As the population grows, deserts are also coming under pressure from people seeking land for homes.

Global warming

The Earth is getting warmer, causing longer dry spells and increasing the risk of wildfires. Both drought and fire have devastating effects on desert plants and animals. For example, these Joshua trees were destroyed by a deadly wildfire in the Mojave Desert.

Storms

As deserts spread, sandstorms and duststorms are becoming more frequent. They don't just affect the desert. Wind carries sand and dust over long distances, causing problems for people and wildlife thousands of kilometres away.

Flooding

In some deserts, flooding is becoming a serious problem. Although heavy rain is rare in these regions, scientists predict it may occur more often as the climate warms, changing weather around the world.

Desertification

In some places, deserts are growing at an alarming rate as people cut down trees for fuelwood and animals overgraze on the few remaining plants. Without roots to hold the soil, it dries out quickly and is easily blown away.

THREATS

Wildlife in danger

With deserts under so much strain, the survival of many desert animals, such as the Dama gazelle and Saharan cheetah, is at risk. Many desert species are so well adapted to their habitats that they cannot survive anywhere else.

Dama gazelle

Saharan cheetah

Controlling damage

Planting more trees is one way to stop deserts from spreading. People are also being encouraged to reduce grazing animals and grow crops instead. This helps improve soil quality and prevents erosion.

25

Hot and dry deserts

Hot and dry deserts have warm, parched conditions throughout the year. Very little rain falls here, and water droplets often evaporate before they even reach the ground. The temperatures are extreme, too. It can be scorching hot during the day and below freezing at night. Some of the world's most famous deserts are identified as hot and dry. They include the Arabian, Sahara, Mojave, Thar, and Great Victoria.

FACT FILE

Area
9 million km² (3.5 million miles²)

Average rainfall
20 to 250 mm (1 to 10 in)

Average temperature
16 to 37°C (61 to 99°F)

Rolling dunes

Wavy seas of sand dunes stretch across a quarter of the Sahara Desert. The dunes mostly range about 20–100 m (65–325 ft) in height. Fierce desert winds sculpt them into different shapes, such as these crescent-shaped barchan dunes.

Sahara Desert

The vast Sahara Desert in northern Africa is the largest hot desert in the world.

Covering about 7 per cent of the Earth's land area, the Sahara Desert is around the same size as the USA. It stretches from the Mediterranean Sea in the north to the Red Sea in the east and the Atlantic Ocean in the west. Soaring temperatures and lack of water make this a challenging ecosystem for animals and plants.

The addax feeds on water-rich plants, such as desert melons.

Harsh habitat

Deserts are tough places to live in because of high temperatures and little water. Many desert animals, such as the addax and barbary sheep, stay in the shade during the day, out of the scorching heat. They become active and set off in search of food when it is cooler, like early morning or late afternoon.

SOME SAHARAN SAND DUNES CAN BE UP TO 465 M (1,525 FT) TALL.

AFRICA

Ancient landscape

Ancient rock art from the plateau of Tassili-n-Ajjer in Algeria shows that the Sahara Desert was once much wetter and greener than it is today. Thousands of years ago, it was home to herds of cattle as well as giraffes, rhinos, and crocodiles.

HOT AND DRY DESERTS

Geography of the Sahara Desert

The Sahara Desert sits on top of a huge area of ancient rocks, known as the African Shield. Experts estimate from the age of these rocks that the Sahara first became a desert around 2-3 million years ago. Over the last few hundred thousand years, the climate of the Sahara has shifted between dry and wet. Its current dry phase is set to last for another 15,000 years.

Landscape

Vast, flat areas of shifting sand dunes cover a quarter of the Sahara Desert. The rest of the desert is rocky. There are also mountain ranges, deep dips called depressions, and salt flats – basins that fill with water when there is a rare shower of rain.

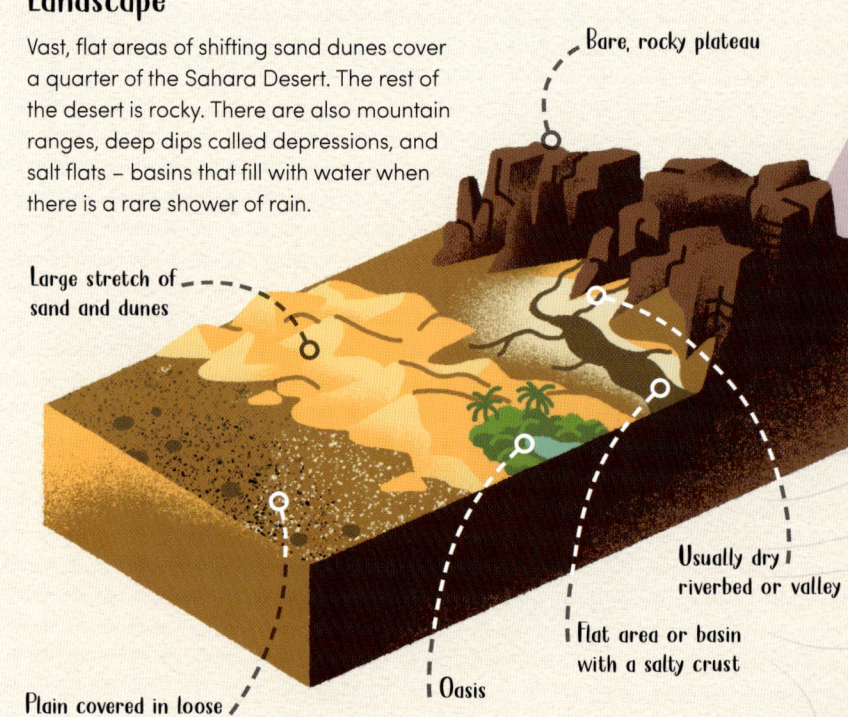

- Bare, rocky plateau
- Large stretch of sand and dunes
- Usually dry riverbed or valley
- Flat area or basin with a salty crust
- Oasis
- Plain covered in loose stones and gravel

SAHARA DESERT

Wild weather

Raging winds regularly blast across the Sahara, whipping up large amounts of dust. Some add to the scorching heat, while others bring cooler air. One such wind, the "harmattan", blows from the Sahara to the Atlantic Ocean from November to mid-March. It can cause temperatures to drop to 9°C (48°F) in some parts of western Africa.

Strong harmattan winds stir up dust and sand.

Desert peaks

The jagged peaks of the Ahaggar Mountains rise around 3,000 m (9,842 ft) from the centre of the Sahara, surrounded by black gravel plains. The rocks making up the peaks and plains are mainly volcanic, produced by eruptions that occurred some 2 million years ago.

Oases

Dotted across the bone-dry desert are pools of water, often surrounded by lush green plants. These oases are formed by water, stored in layers of rocks under the sand, which rises to the surface. These are a welcome sight for desert travellers – animals or humans.

HOT AND DRY DESERTS

Animals of the Sahara Desert

Jerboa
(Jaculus jaculus)

During the day, the tiny jerboa stays cool in its underground burrow. At night, it comes out to look for seeds and insects to eat. It can hop long distances on its strong back legs, using its tail for balance.

Despite the harsh conditions, the Sahara Desert is home to an amazing range of animals, many of which are found nowhere else on Earth. They include around 70 species of mammals, 90 species of birds, and 100 species of reptiles, as well as many insects and other smaller creatures. Special features allow these animals to survive the extreme heat and lack of water.

Fat-tailed scorpion
(Androctonus australis)

At the tip of this scorpion's thick, powerful tail is a stinger that injects deadly venom into prey. The scorpion's outer covering, or exoskeleton, is tough enough to protect it from desert sandstorms, which are fierce enough to strip paint off a car!

Carrying water

For desert animals, finding enough water can be tough, especially when they have young. Sandgrouse have a clever solution. The male visits a water hole and soaks its belly feathers in the water. It carries water back to its nest for the chicks to drink.

The sandgrouse lies in the water until its feathers are soaking wet.

Sandfish
(Scincus scincus)

This desert lizard appears to "swim" through sand. To escape the heat, a sandfish dives headfirst into the sand, with its legs tucked into the sides. Then, it wriggles its body from side to side to move forwards.

Its wide, powerful body helps the sandfish move under thick layers of sand.

Addax
(Addax nasomaculatus)

A shy, stocky antelope, the addax lives in small herds among the sand dunes. It rests in the shade during the hottest part of the day and is mostly active at night. The addax gets most of its water from the desert plants it eats.

Fennec fox
(Vulpes zerda)

Known for its huge, fluffy ears, this little fox is perfectly adapted to desert life. At night, its super-sized ears help listen for prey, such as insects, rodents, and lizards. The ears also allow the fox to stay cool by giving off heat.

Horned viper
(Cerastes cerastes)

Lying half-buried in the sand, a deadly venomous horned viper is almost impossible to spot. Its mottled, light-brown scales blend in perfectly with the sand, with only its "horns" poking out. The viper waits patiently for an unsuspecting mouse or bird to pass by, then it strikes.

HOT AND DRY DESERTS

Dromedary camel

The one-humped dromedary, or Arabian camel, is found in the Sahara and Arabian deserts. Superbly adapted to desert life, dromedaries are able to travel long distances without needing water and food. This has made them an essential mode of transport for people living in the desert.

Mouth
A camel will happily munch on desert plants that are too prickly for other animals. Its lips and tongue are large and tough, and its mouth is lined with fleshy bumps that prevent the prickles from scratching or causing other injuries.

SAHARA DESERT

In a sandstorm, camels close their nostrils to stop sand getting into their nose.

Feet
Walking across soft sand can be tricky and tiring, especially for an animal weighing as much as 650 kg (1,433 lb). To avoid sinking, camels have large, round feet with two spread-out toes that help distribute their weight evenly over the ground.

Eyes
To keep sand and dust out of their large eyes, camels have bushy eyebrows and two sets of very long eyelashes. They also have extra eyelids that sweep across their eyes to clean them, like the windscreen wipers on a car.

Hump
Camels store fat in their humps, which they can convert into water and energy when there is nothing else to eat or drink. Dromedaries have one hump, while Bactrian camels from the Gobi Desert have two.

35

HOT AND DRY DESERTS

Sahara's sweet tree
Towering date palm trees are a familiar sight in the Sahara, growing around oases. For thousands of years, they have played a vital part in desert life. People eat their sweet fruit, turn their large leaves into baskets and mats, build houses and bridges with their trunks, and make ropes using their tough fibres.

Plants of the Sahara Desert

Large stretches of the Sahara appear far too dry for plants to grow. Yet, scattered across the desert – in mountain valleys, on salt flats, and even on sand dunes – a surprising variety of plants have found ways to thrive. A range of survival features, including long roots and small, thick leaves, allow them to make the most of any water around.

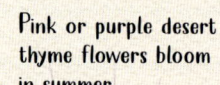

Pink or purple desert thyme flowers bloom in summer.

Laperrine's olive tree
(Olea europaea laperrini)

It is hard to imagine olives growing in a desert, but some of the olive trees found in the Sahara may be thousands of years old. These trees are related to the olive trees grown in Mediterranean countries, and are valued for their wood by the desert communities.

Waxy leaves help cut down water loss.

Giant milkweed
(Calotropis procera)

Giant milkweed is a desert shrub with thick, fleshy leaves, and a secret weapon. If any part of the plant is cut or broken, it oozes milky-white sap. The sap quickly turns rubbery, and is highly toxic to people and animals.

Saharan cypress
(Cupressus dupreziana)

This rare species of cypress is native to the Tassili-n-Ajjer mountains in Algeria, with fewer than 250 known trees. The largest and oldest among them is called Tin-Balalan, which measures about 12 m (40 ft) wide and is more than 2,000 years old.

Bitter apple
(Citrullus colocynthis)

Also known as the desert melon, or bitter cucumber, this plant takes root in dunes and has long, vine-like stems that spread across the sand. It grows hard, round fruit that look like small watermelons but have a bitter taste.

Desert thyme
(Thymus vulgaris)

Thyme was brought from Europe to be cultivated in Africa a long time ago. This low-growing herb has small, grey-green leaves. It needs very little water and thrives in the hot, sunny parts of the Sahara, where it forms thick, sweet-smelling clumps. Thyme is often used to flavour food.

Desert duststorm

Whipped up by strong winds, a huge, billowing wall of dust hurtles across the desert – a duststorm is on its way. The wall can reach 1.6 km (1 mile) high and measure 160 km (100 miles) across. Fine dust covers everything in its path, making it difficult to see or breathe. Once it is high in the air, the dust can be carried to places thousands of kilometres away.

FACT FILE

Area
140,000 km² (54,000 miles²)

Average rainfall
50 to 125 mm (2 to 5 in)

Average temperature
−13 to 48°C (8 to 120°F)

NORTH AMERICA

Mojave Desert

Named after the Mojave people, the Mojave Desert is the USA's smallest desert.

Lying mostly in the state of California, the Mojave Desert also reaches into Nevada, Arizona, and Utah. Together with the Sonoran, Chihuahuan, and Great Basin deserts, it makes up the larger North American desert. The Great Basin lies to the north of the Mojave, the Sonoran to the south. To the west, the Mojave borders the Sierra Nevada mountains and to the east is the Colorado River.

Tough plants
Like desert plants everywhere, those found in the Mojave need to be strong to survive. Cacti, such as this beavertail cactus, also offer much-needed food and shelter to birds, lizards, and other desert animals.

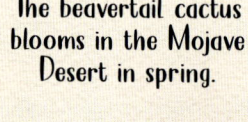
The beavertail cactus blooms in the Mojave Desert in spring.

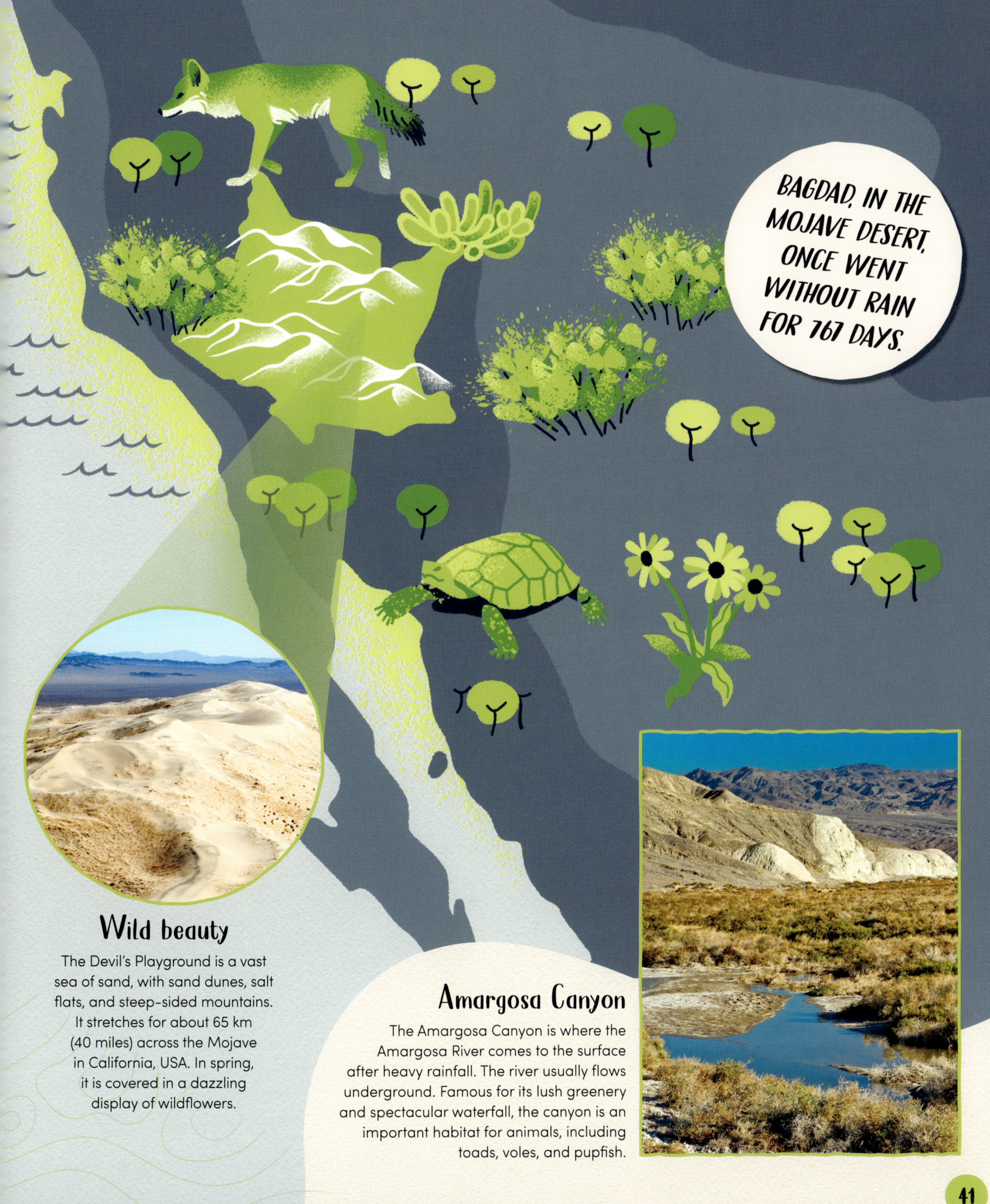

BAGDAD, IN THE MOJAVE DESERT, ONCE WENT WITHOUT RAIN FOR 767 DAYS.

Wild beauty

The Devil's Playground is a vast sea of sand, with sand dunes, salt flats, and steep-sided mountains. It stretches for about 65 km (40 miles) across the Mojave in California, USA. In spring, it is covered in a dazzling display of wildflowers.

Amargosa Canyon

The Amargosa Canyon is where the Amargosa River comes to the surface after heavy rainfall. The river usually flows underground. Famous for its lush greenery and spectacular waterfall, the canyon is an important habitat for animals, including toads, voles, and pupfish.

HOT AND DRY DESERTS

Basin and range

The Mojave is known as a basin-and-range desert. This means it is made up of flat valleys, called basins, alternating with tall mountains, or ranges. Millions of years ago, these mountains were forced up between giant cracks, called faults, in the Earth's crust.

Climate contrasts

Summers in the Mojave are baking hot, with thunderstorms and heavy showers that can cause flash flooding. By contrast, winters are freezing cold, with strong winds blowing in from the Pacific Ocean, as well as rain and snow in the mountains.

Geography of the Mojave Desert

Most of the Mojave Desert lies at a high altitude. This has a major effect on its climate – it is cooler and wetter higher up. Mountains are also one of the reasons why the desert is so dry. The Sierra Nevada and Transvere ranges block clouds blowing in from the Pacific Ocean, forcing them to drop their rain before it can reach the desert.

Unusual rock formations

Dramatic rock formations, like the one below, can be found scattered across the Mojave landscape. They date back to around 100 million years ago when magma from deep underground oozed to the surface, cooling on its way up.

Wind and flash floods carved the rocks into their odd shapes.

A bajada in the Mojave Desert

Features

At the base of the mountains lie broad, fan-shaped slopes of gravel. In the Mojave, these are known as bajadas. Made up of sediment washed down from the mountains, they can spread out thousands of metres into the surrounding desert.

Animals of the Mojave Desert

With sandy plains, salt flats, and high mountains, the Mojave offers a wide range of habitats for hundreds of animals. Some are full-time residents, while others stop by as they travel from place to place. Bighorn sheep and jackrabbits are found all over Mojave, but salamanders and pupfish survive in just a few rare spots.

Desert long-horned grasshopper
(Tanaocerus koebelei)

Mostly found on the ground, these desert insects have fine antennae or "horns" longer than their bodies, and powerful back legs for jumping. Perfectly camouflaged against the sand and gravel, they stay hidden from predators.

Coyote
(Canis latrans)

Closely related to wolves, coyotes are superbly adjusted to desert life. They eat whatever is available – hunting rodents and rabbits, scavenging on carrion (dead animals), and feasting on prickly pears. Clever and sociable, they live in family groups, communicating with howls, yips, and barks.

Desert tortoise
(Gopherus agassizii)

A desert tortoise escapes the heat by spending most of its life underground. It can survive for a whole year without water. When it does find water, however, it can drink enough in one go to increase its body weight by almost a half.

MOJAVE DESERT

Sidewinder
(Crotalus cerastes)

This snake moves its body sideways in wide loops to avoid overheating. During the day, it buries itself beneath the sand or rocks. The small horns above its eyes help keep sand away. At night, the snake emerges to hunt for rodents and lizards.

Greater roadrunner
(Geococcyx californianus)

One of the quirkiest-looking birds in the Mojave, the roadrunner is famous for feasting on venomous rattlesnakes and scorpions. It also snacks on lizards, rodents, bats, and other birds. A roadrunner chases its prey on its long legs, even though it can fly short distances.

Gila monster
(Heloderma suspectum)

Since food is hard to find, a gila monster can eat a third of its body weight in one meal. It also stores fat in its sausage-like tail for times when food is scarce or during cold winter months when it mostly stays underground.

The gila flicks its forked tongue out to smell food, such as tortoise eggs and rabbits.

Pond dweller

You might not expect to find fish in the Mojave but pupfish have lived there for thousands of years. Today, however, they survive only in a few isolated pools – what's left of a network of large lakes that covered the desert millions of years ago.

HOT AND DRY DESERTS

Plants of the Mojave Desert

An astonishing variety of plants and trees grow in the Mojave, despite the harsh conditions. Among them are tall Joshua trees, prickly cacti, and delicate wildflowers – all adapted to survive down on the dry, sandy plains or higher up in the mountains. About a quarter of these plant species only grow in the Mojave.

Desert holly
(Atriplex hymenelytra)

With its spiky leaves and small, red fruit, this desert shrub might look like the holly you put up at Christmas, although the two are not related. Desert holly is a type of saltbush – one of the very few plants that can live and grow in salty soil.

The desert holly grows clumps of brownish flowers.

Beavertail cactus
(Opuntia basiliaris)

The beavertail cactus is a small, low-growing cactus that sprouts dark pink flowers in spring. Instead of stems and leaves, it has hundreds of flat, fleshy pads, that look like beaver tails. The pads are designed for storing spare supplies of water.

Brittlebush
(Encelia farinosa)

The leaves of a brittlebush are covered in thick, silvery hairs that reflect sunlight. This helps the plant stay cool and trap moisture. During particularly cold or dry times of the year, the brittlebush sheds its leaves to save water and energy.

Teddy-bear cholla
(Cylindropuntia bigelovii)
It may look like it's covered in soft, fluffy fur, but this cactus is no teddy bear. The "fur" is very long and spiny, with dangerous barbs capable of sticking into skin. Despite this, animals like antelope squirrels clamber over the cactus to feed on its fruit.

Creosote bush
(Larrea tridentata)
Found in the driest parts of the desert, this evergreen shrub is as tough as it gets. Its roots grow deep down to reach water, spreading out for many metres. Chemicals found in the roots prevent other plants from growing too close and tapping into its water supply.

Brightly coloured leaves, called bracts, surround the dull green flowers.

Deep roots
One of the most useful plants in the Mojave is the mesquite, which grows a long root up to 25 m (82 ft) to reach underground water. This allows it to survive in the hottest, driest parts in the desert, where it provides animals with food, shelter, and shade.

Desert paintbrush
(Castilleja chromosa)
Many plants use large, showy flowers to attract pollinators, such as insects and birds. The desert paintbrush, with its tiny greenish flowers, might be easily overlooked, but its dazzling red leaves catch the visitors' attention.

HOT AND DRY DESERTS

Joshua tree

With tall trunks and spreading branches, Joshua trees are a striking sight. The most famous plants in the Mojave, they even have their own national park. Like many desert plants, Joshua trees grow slowly and can live for around 150 years, though some may be much older. Despite their name, they are not trees but giant yucca plants that can reach heights of up to 12 m (40 ft).

Food and nests

This Scott's oriole is one of the many bird species that rely on the Joshua tree. It feeds on the plant's flowers and fruit, and builds its nest among the spiky leaves. Other animals also seek shelter nearby – Yucca night lizards can be found poking around the tree's base, searching for insects to eat.

MOJAVE DESERT

Trunk
A Joshua tree has a single trunk that grows to about 1 m (3 ft) tall before branching out. Unlike a "real tree" its trunk isn't woody, but is made up of thousands of small bundles of strong fibres. The fibres support the tree, as well as store water.

The flowers are greenish-white and have a waxy texture.

Leaves
The green leaves are long, stiff, and sharply pointed. They grow in spiky clusters at the ends of branches. Dead leaves cling to the trunk and branches, helping shield the tree from the sun and reduce water loss.

Flowers
In spring, bunches of flowers bloom at the tips of branches, but only if conditions are right. Cool temperatures and ample rain help the flowers open. Yucca moths pollinate the flowers while laying their eggs inside. The newly hatched larvae feed on seeds.

Death Valley

Close to the border with the Great Basin Desert is the terrifying-sounding Death Valley. It lies in a basin around 225 km (140 miles) long. At up to 85 m (280 ft) below sea level, Death Valley is the lowest point in the USA. It is also the hottest and driest, with the highest ever air temperature recorded at 57°C (134°F) on 10 July 1913.

THE NAME "THAR" COMES FROM A LOCAL WORD FOR "SAND".

The Aravallis

The rugged Aravalli Hills form the south-eastern border of the Thar. Some of the oldest mountains in India, they date back to around 670 million years ago. By blocking winds carrying moisture, the Aravallis play a huge part in the desert staying dry.

Sam Sand Dunes

Vast stretches of dunes sweep across large parts of the Thar. Among the most dramatic are the Sam Sand Dunes, not far from the ancient city of Jaisalmer in Rajasthan, India. At sunset, the sand glows pink, orange, and gold, as if it has been painted.

FACT FILE

Area
200,000 km² (77,220 miles²)

Average rainfall
100 to 500 mm (4 to 20 in)

Average temperature
0 to 49°C (32 to 120°F)

Khejri trees can survive temperatures from cool to scorching hot.

The iconic Khejri
Among the many plant species found in the Thar, the khejri tree stands out. Able to grow in the harshest conditions, it provides food and shade for people and animals. It also offers the perfect perch for the majestic peacock.

Thar Desert

Also known as the Great Indian Desert, the Thar is an enormous, sandy desert located mostly in northwest India and Pakistan.

The Thar Desert rolls out in waves of sand, bordered by river plains and mountain ranges. It is the most densely populated desert in the world. Most of the people living in the Thar are farmers growing crops, such as wheat and cotton. Thousands of tourists also visit the desert every year to explore its ancient cities and impressive landscapes.

HOT AND DRY DESERTS

Geography of the Thar Desert

Millions of years ago, the Thar Desert was a very different place. At times, huge rivers flowed across the region but later dried up, leaving salt flats and sand dunes behind. However, strong, sand-carrying winds only began to blow around 200,000 years ago, giving the dry desert conditions we know today.

Sea of sand

While many deserts are over 5 million years old, the sand covering the Thar has been built up over the past 1.8 million years only. This makes it one of the youngest deserts in the world. The sand is constantly shifting, blown by the strong desert winds.

Desert islands

Isolated hills, called inselbergs, rise from flat desert plains. Made of plugs, or funnel-shaped masses, of hard volcanic rock, these islands can form slowly over millions of years.

A plug of hard volcanic rock lies underground.

Water and wind erode, or wear away, the surrounding softer rock, making the hard rock appear taller.

Over time, erosion shapes the exposed rock into an inselberg.

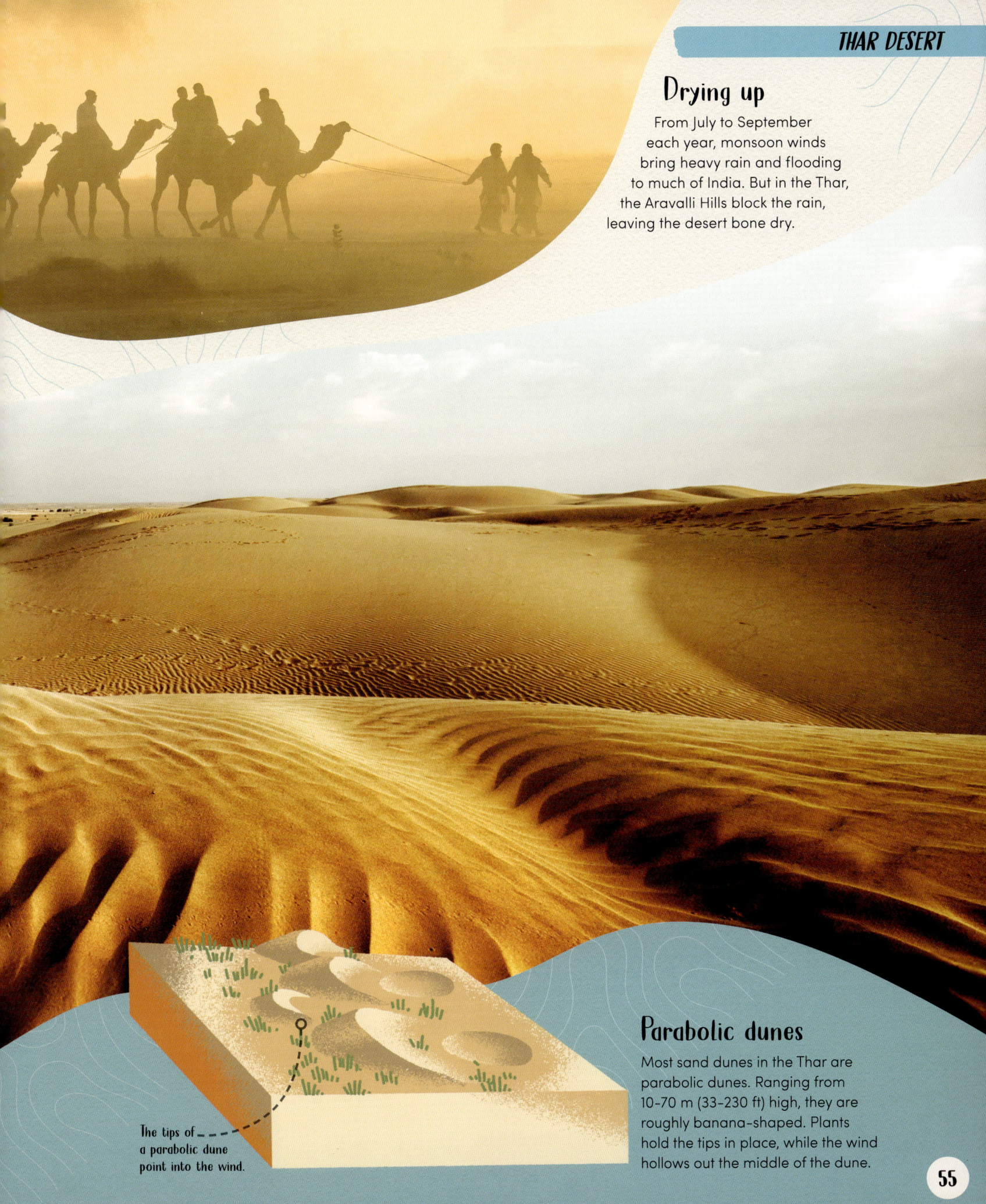

THAR DESERT

Drying up

From July to September each year, monsoon winds bring heavy rain and flooding to much of India. But in the Thar, the Aravalli Hills block the rain, leaving the desert bone dry.

Parabolic dunes

Most sand dunes in the Thar are parabolic dunes. Ranging from 10–70 m (33–230 ft) high, they are roughly banana-shaped. Plants hold the tips in place, while the wind hollows out the middle of the dune.

The tips of a parabolic dune point into the wind.

HOT AND DRY DESERTS

Animals of the Thar Desert

At first glance, the Thar Desert might look empty and lifeless. Lack of water, harsh winds, and scorching daytime temperatures make this a tough habitat. Yet, the Thar is home to hundreds of animal species. They include mammals, such as the chinkara and Indian wild ass, that are fast disappearing elsewhere in India.

Indian desert jird
(Meriones hurrianae)

Gerbil-like jirds dig burrows in sandy ground. In summer, they come out at dawn and dusk to feed, then spend the hottest parts of the day underground. In winter, they stay above the ground during the day, then head back to their burrows at night when the temperature drops.

Caracal
(Caracal caracal)

Also known as a desert lynx, the caracal uses its large, tufted ears to detect prey at night. A skilful hunter, this athletic wild cat can leap high into the air on its strong back legs to catch birds in mid-flight.

Caracals twitch their long ears to communicate with others.

Sand wasp
(Steniolia sp/Bembicidae family)

To spot a sand wasp, look for a burst of sand flying backwards – kicked up as it digs its tube-like burrow in a dune. At the end of the burrow is a nesting chamber where the wasp lays its eggs.

Sand snake
(Psammophis schokari)

With a long, thin body and dark brown stripes, this snake is camouflaged in the sand to hunt prey and avoid predators. Also known as the whip snake for its speed, it chases rodents and lizards across the ground and climbs trees to reach birds and their eggs.

Indian fringe-toed lizard
(Acanthodactylus cantoris)
To escape from snakes and other predators, this lizard dives headfirst into the sand and disappears. It can also run quickly along the surface. The lizard gets its name from the rows of fringe-like scales on its back toes, which help it grip loose sand.

Chinkara
(Gazella bennettii)
Measuring about 0.6 m (2 ft) tall, chinkaras are small antelopes with long, ringed horns. They are active at night when they search for food and can go for days without water – surviving on dew and moisture from the plants they eat.

Migratory birds
Each year, large numbers of birds stop in the Thar Desert, on their way between their breeding and feeding grounds. Among them are thousands of demoiselle cranes that gather in huge, noisy flocks near village ponds and other water sources to spend the winter.

HOT AND DRY DESERTS

Features

Great Indian bustards have a distinctive appearance – with a brown back and wings, white belly and neck, and a crest of black feathers on top of their heads. Males have larger crests than females, along with bands of black feathers across their breasts.

Eggs

Once a year, the female lays a single egg in the open, in a shallow hole called a scrape. It takes about a month for the chick to hatch, and another month before it is ready to fly. During this time, the mother guards it from predators, such as foxes and lizards.

Great Indian bustard

Stalking slowly across the scrubby desert ground, the great Indian bustard is a magnificent sight. With its long neck and legs, this huge bird can stand more than 1 m (3 ft) tall. It weighs up to 15 kg (33 lb), making it one of the heaviest flying birds in the world. Though capable of flight, it often struggles to take off due to its weight.

THAR DESERT

A bustard egg is about the size of four hen eggs combined.

Behaviour

Bustards spend most of their time on the ground, foraging for food. They are not fussy eaters and will eat whatever they can find. Depending on the time of year, they feast on grasshoppers, rodents, lizards, berries, and grass seeds.

HOT AND DRY DESERTS

Plants of the Thar Desert

The most common plants in the Thar are thorny trees and tough grasses. They grow in scattered patches across the desert, on both rocky hillsides and sandy dunes. Some even spread over dune slopes and crests. The plants provide food and shelter for animals, as well as fuel and medicines for local people.

Leafless spurge
(Euphorbia caducifolia)

The leafless spurge is a giant, cactus-like plant with many tall stems. In summer, it grows two fleshy leaves at the tips of its stems and clusters of bright red flowers. Animals, such as rodents and lizards, shelter among its thorny stems.

Khejri
(Prosopis cineraria)

This hardy tree has small leaves to reduce water loss and roots that grow up to 30 m (100 ft) deep to reach underground water. It can survive extreme temperature changes, strong winds, and long droughts, making it well suited to the desert.

Stabilizing sand dunes

Dunes in the Thar are always shifting, threatening to cover villages, farms, and roads. To prevent this, rows of tamarisk trees are planted close together in the sand. Their long roots intertwine underground, holding the sand in place.

Desert teak
(Tecomella undulata)

Also known as "rohido", the desert teak tree has vibrant red, orange, or yellow trumpet-shaped flowers that bloom in late winter or early spring. It is valued for its high-quality wood, which is used by locals for building, carving, and making furniture.

Acacia
(Senegalia senegal)

The acacia, or gum Arabic tree, can grow to a height of 5–12 m (16–40 ft). This small, thorny tree can survive long droughts. It bears yellowish-white flowers, and its greyish-white bark is cut to collect gum, which is used as a food additive.

Sewan grass
(Lasiurus scindicus)

This sturdy plant grows in bushy clumps in the sand and can survive for 4–5 years without water. It has thin stems, narrow leaves, and long spikes of hairy flowers. People in the Thar use sewan grass to feed their animals.

White flowers bloom at the end of the stems.

Kheer kheemp
(Cynanchum acidum)

Found on rocky hillsides and outcrops in the Thar Desert, this plant has lots of green stems but no leaves. Since leaves lose water through their surface, going without them is a key survival tactic shared by many desert plants.

Lake Sambhar

Lake Sambhar is the largest of several salt lakes found in the Thar Desert. Its crust of white salt gleams brightly in the sun, streaked with pink, orange, and green. These colours are produced by algae and bacteria that grow in the lake. Only 3 m (10 ft) at its deepest, the lake is an important wintering ground for migratory birds, including thousands of flamingos.

FACT FILE

Area
2.3 million km² (900,000 miles²)

Average rainfall
50 to 200 mm (2 to 8 in)

Average temperature
0 to 49°C (32 to 120°F)

Arabian Desert

In the hot, dry Arabian Desert, great seas of sand stretch as far as the eye can see.

Situated in the far southwest corner of Asia, the Arabian Desert covers almost the entire Arabian Peninsula and lies mostly in the country of Saudi Arabia. The desert reaches from Syria in the north to Yemen and Oman in the south. It is the largest desert in Asia and the fourth-largest on Earth, after the two polar deserts and the Sahara.

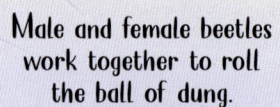

Male and female beetles work together to roll the ball of dung.

Dung beetles

Using their back feet, dung beetles shape animal dung into a ball. Then, they push the ball to a safe place and the female lays her eggs in it. This ensures that when young beetles hatch, they have a ready supply of dung to feed on.

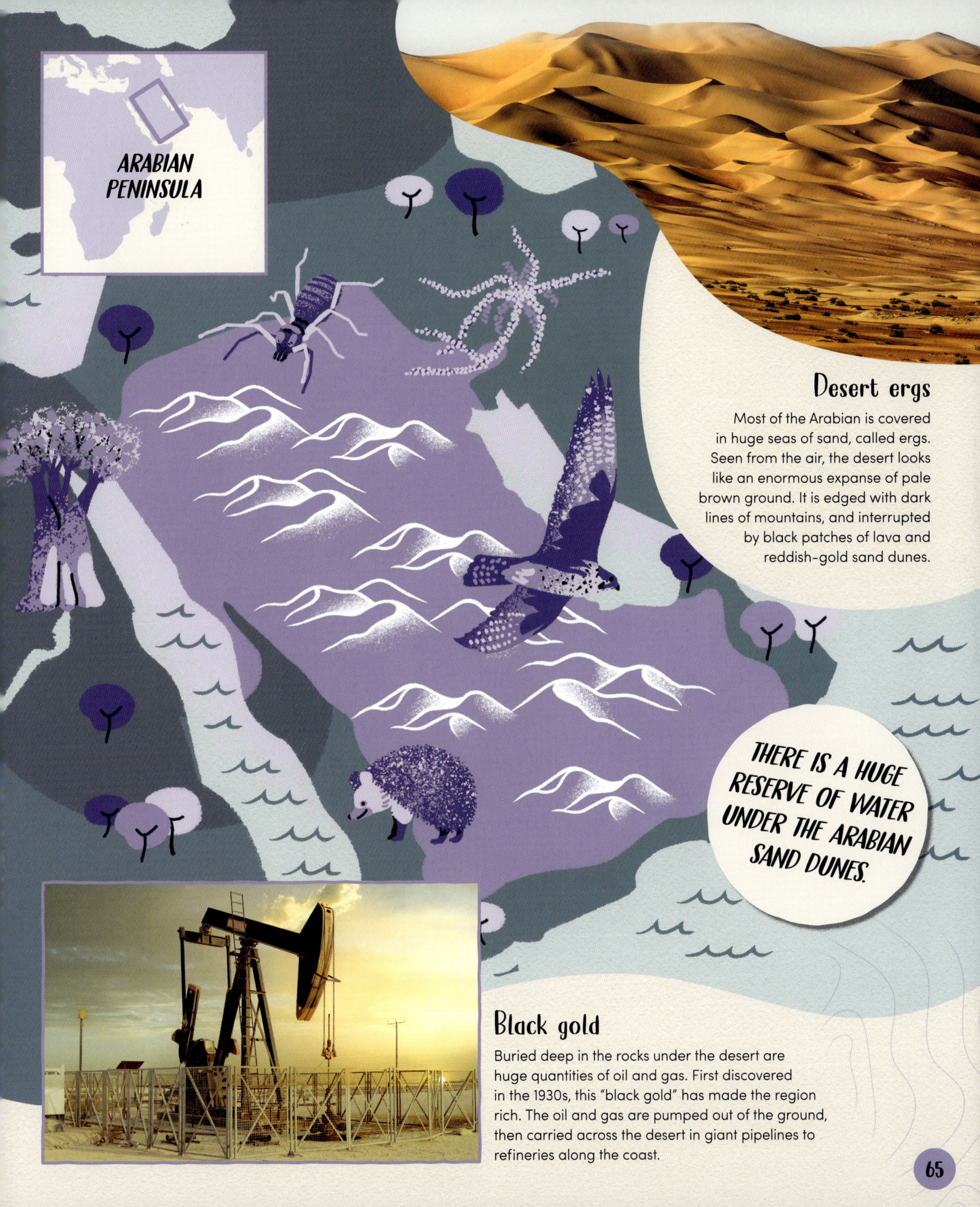

ARABIAN PENINSULA

Desert ergs

Most of the Arabian is covered in huge seas of sand, called ergs. Seen from the air, the desert looks like an enormous expanse of pale brown ground. It is edged with dark lines of mountains, and interrupted by black patches of lava and reddish-gold sand dunes.

THERE IS A HUGE RESERVE OF WATER UNDER THE ARABIAN SAND DUNES.

Black gold

Buried deep in the rocks under the desert are huge quantities of oil and gas. First discovered in the 1930s, this "black gold" has made the region rich. The oil and gas are pumped out of the ground, then carried across the desert in giant pipelines to refineries along the coast.

HOT AND DRY DESERTS

Flash floods

The desert is also dotted with dry river valleys carved into the mountainsides, called wadis. If there is a sudden downpour, the wadis can overflow within minutes. The water turns into raging torrents, causing flash floods that sweep away everything in their path.

Geography of the Arabian Desert

The Arabian Peninsula is a large area of land with water on almost all sides. Millions of years ago, it was joined to the continent of Africa until movements of the Earth's crust caused it to split away. Today, the Arabian Desert covers most of the peninsula. While much of the desert is sandy, there are also mountains, cliffs, valleys, gravel plains, and salt flats.

Volcanic desert

Some parts of the Arabian Desert are covered in massive dark patches of lava that erupted from volcanoes over millions of years ago. In Arabic, these lava fields are known as "harrat", meaning "stony places burned by fire".

ARABIAN DESERT

Asir Mountains

The Asir Mountains stretch along the southwestern edge of the Arabian Desert, running parallel to the Red Sea. The ecosystem here is cooler and wetter than the surrounding desert, providing a home for many rare animals, such as baboons, ibex, and leopards.

Light from the sky
Layer of cool air
Layer of warm air
Light rays bend towards cooler air.
To the observer, it appears as a reflection on the ground.

Seeing things

In the dry areas of the desert, a pool of water is a welcome sight. But is the water really there, or is it a mirage? Mirages are caused by layers of warm and cool air bending light coming from above. What you actually see is not water, but a reflection of the sky.

HOT AND DRY DESERTS

Arabian fat-tailed scorpion
(Androctonus crassicauda)
This deadly scorpion grows to about 10 cm (4 in) long and has a thick, curved tail. By day, it hides in rock crevices. At night, it comes out to hunt for food, such as insects and lizards. The scorpion grabs prey with its pincers, then flips the tail forwards to inject a lethal dose of venom.

Desert hedgehog
(Paraechinus aethiopicus)
To survive in the desert, this little hedgehog usually gets water from the insects and other creatures it eats. During very hot or dry times, it aestivates (slows down or becomes inactive) in its burrow to save water and energy.

Saker falcon
(Falco cherrug)
Flying fast above the desert, a saker falcon scans the ground for prey, such as rodents or birds. When the falcon spots one, it snatches the prey with its sharp, curved talons and tears it apart with its strong, hooked beak.

The saker falcon has a wingspan of 100-110 cm (40-43 in).

Animals of the Arabian Desert

From rugged mountains to sandy plains, the Arabian Desert hosts a wide range of habitats and a remarkable variety of animals. These include mammals like Ruppell's foxes, reptiles such as sand cobras, insects like butterflies, and birds such as kestrels. The region also lies along a key migration route for birds travelling between Asia and Africa.

Camel spider
(Galeodes arabs)

Camel spiders are fierce predators, with one-third of their body made up of large, powerful jaws. They dine on insects, lizards, and rodents – grabbing and chomping them into a pulp. Despite their name, camel spiders are not known to attack camels.

Survival instincts

The desert white butterfly lives in the driest part of the Arabian Desert. To survive, it speeds up or slows down its life cycle until conditions are right for laying eggs. It can stay as a pupa for years, while most butterflies remain in that stage for only a few weeks.

Dabb
(Uromastyx aegyptia)

By day, a dabb feeds on flowers and fruit, making it an easy target for snakes and birds of prey. Some predators are put off by the sight of its spiny tail. For others, the dab dives into its burrow, lashing its tail from side to side as a warning.

Dung beetle
(Scarabaeus sacer)

Dung beetles scurry after herds of sheep and camels, ready to pounce on fresh droppings to roll into dung balls. They may travel long distances, antennae twitching, in search of the perfect pat of dung.

HOT AND DRY DESERTS

Herd

Oryxes are social animals that live in herds of up to 30. In hard conditions, they break into smaller groups to stand a better chance of finding food. A herd is usually made up of males, females, and their young – a baby oryx can stand and walk just an hour after being born.

Coat

An oryx's bright white coat reflects the sun's rays, allowing it to stay cool on hot days. In winter, the coat and legs turn darker to keep it warm, as dark colours absorb heat.

Arabian oryx

Arabian oryxes are antelopes that are about 1 m (3 ft) tall. During the day, they rest in shallow scrapes, or hollows in the sand, where it is cooler. They become active at dawn and dusk. Around 50 years ago, there were no wild oryxes left. So many had been killed by hunters, they were declared extinct. Some zoos helped raise baby oryxes and then released them back into the desert.

Both male and female oryxes have long, slender, and sharply pointed horns.

Hooves

An oryx has wide, spread-out hooves. While they look a bit big for its body, the hooves help the oryx walk easily on soft sand. It also uses its front hooves like shovels to dig scrapes in the sand.

A special circulatory system in the oryx's head helps to cool its blood.

Diet

Oryxes mainly graze on plants, which provide both food and water. They can smell rain from kilometers away. Oryxes also walk long distances to feed on new plants that may have sprouted in the wet land.

Plants of the Arabian Desert

The diverse landscapes of the Arabian Desert support a rich array of plant life. Large expanses of sand are too dry for most plants to grow, except for hardy shrubs and grasses. Higher up in the mountains and wadis there is enough water to support acacia, juniper, and tamarisk trees. Colourful wildflowers bloom quickly after rare bursts of rain.

Juniper
(Juniperus procera)

Thick forests of juniper trees grow on mountain slopes, where conditions are cooler and wetter. These trees have bright green, needle-like leaves and bluish-black, berry-like cones. A variety of birds, including thrushes and warblers, can be found among the branches of these trees.

Desert rose
(Adenium obesum)

Named after its rose-like flowers, this plant stands strong against the desert's unforgiving climate. It is a succulent plant, meaning it stores water in its thick, trunk-like stem. The plant's small, leathery leaves help reduce water loss, and in dry, cold weather, it can even shed them to conserve moisture.

The shrub produces clusters of tiny orange flowers.

Had
(Cornulaca monocantha)

Also known as the prickly saltwort, had is a type of shrub that grows on sandy or stony ground. It has wiry stems, stubby leaves, and small, black seeds that grow in pods. Each leaf ends in a stiff spine. The plant is well adapted to strong winds.

ARABIAN DESERT

Panic grass
(Panicum turgidum)
This desert grass grows in thick clumps on dunes and salt flats. Some stems grow sideways and take root in the sand, forming new plants. This spreads the grass faster than growing from seeds.

Firebush
(Calligonum comosum)
The firebush grows on dune slopes, where its roots help hold the loose sand in place. Reaching up to 2 m (6 ft) tall, it has stiff, spiky stems with tiny leaves. In spring, the firebush produces small, sweet-smelling flowers, followed by hairy red or yellow fruit.

Ahneh has long stamens – the parts of flowers that produce pollen for making seeds.

Ahneh
(Teucrium oliverianum)
Ahneh is a small, ground-hugging shrub that grows in wadis and on gravel plains. It has triangular green leaves and eye-catching violet flowers that bloom in spring. Ahneh does well in sandy or rocky desert soil, but cannot cope with overly salty ground.

Salty conditions
Most plants struggle to grow in salty ground, as too much salt can be deadly. But the desert saltbush is an exception. Its tiny hairy leaves help remove excess salt, preventing build-up inside the plant. The salt gives the leaves a grey colour.

Rub' al-Khali

At the centre of the Arabian Desert lies the Rub' al-Khali. Covering around 660,000 km^2 (250,000 miles^2), this gigantic sand sea is about the size of France. Its name means "Empty Quarter" because its climate is too hostile for people to live there. It's famous for its sand dunes, including the long, straight seif dunes that stretch to more than 250 km (155 miles).

Serpentine Lakes

The Serpentine Lakes is a string of desert salt lakes that runs for around 100 km (60 miles) along the border between Western and South Australia. Usually dry and covered in a salty crust, the lakes can fill with water after heavy rain.

OVER 100 SPECIES OF REPTILES LIVE IN THE GREAT VICTORIA DESERT.

Red sand dunes

Flaming red sand dunes cover large parts of the Great Victoria. The sand gets its colour from iron oxide – the same chemical that turns metal rusty. Iron oxide was formed over millions of years as iron in desert rocks reacted with oxygen in the air.

AUSTRALIA

FACT FILE

Area
338,500 km² (130,700 miles²)

Average rainfall
150 to 250 mm (6 to 10 in)

Average temperature
18 to 40°C (64 to 104°F)

A gum tree's leaves and branches offer much-needed shade and home for animals.

Great Victoria Desert

Australia's largest desert, the Great Victoria is a sunbaked land of rolling sand dunes and glittering salt lakes.

The Great Victoria Desert stretches from Western Australia to South Australia and has several national parks and reserves. It runs for some 700 km (440 miles) from west to east. Dry, parched land surrounds it – there are deserts to the north and east, scrubland to the west, and the vast, stony Nullarbor Plain to the south.

River red gum

These trees are easily recognized by their creamy white bark, which peels to reveal red, brown, or grey. Found along dry riverbeds and creeks, their deep roots draw water from the ground. They can also shed most of their leaves during droughts.

HOT AND DRY DESERTS

Geography of the Great Victoria Desert

About one-third of Australia is covered in desert, making it the driest inhabited continent. Millions of years ago, it was part of a much larger continent, called Gondwanaland. When Gondwanaland broke apart, Australia drifted north and became much drier. Today, it has 10 named deserts – the Great Victoria is the largest.

Lunette dunes

A striking feature of the Great Victoria is its crescent-shaped lunette, or "little moon", dunes. They are formed when sand and clay blow from dry lake beds. Unlike most types of sand dune, a lunette dune stays fixed in place at the lake edge, stretching for up to 6.5 km (4 miles).

Climate

Summers, from December to February, in the Great Victoria are very hot. During winters, from June to August, the night temperatures fall below freezing, with occasional winter frosts. A few water holes form along creek beds after rare rainfall. These water holes are vital for wildlife during the dry season.

GREAT VICTORIA DESERT

Salt lakes

Many dry salt lakes, or playas, are found in the eastern part of the Great Victoria. They fill with water only after heavy rain. However, since these lakes are usually shallow, the water quickly evaporates in the desert heat, leaving a layer of salt behind.

Desert pavements

Desert pavements, also known as gibber plains, cover large parts of the Great Victoria. They are made from closely packed pebbles and stones, shaped by erosion over millions of years. They are coated in "desert varnish" – a thin, shiny layer of dark red or brown clay.

Wind and rain remove sand and dust from the surface.

This leaves larger stones and pebbles behind.

They form a desert pavement, or gibber plain.

HOT AND DRY DESERTS

Scarlet-chested parrot
(Neophema splendida)

The rainbow colours of the scarlet-chested parrots make a dazzling sight. These colourful birds fly across the desert in small flocks, looking for grass seeds to eat. They can go long periods without drinking, getting most of their water from plants.

Southern marsupial mole
(Notoryctes typhlops)

With spade-like front paws and a cone-shaped head, this unusual animal is built for burrowing. It spends most of its life beneath the sand, going as deep as 1 m (3 ft). The mole mostly feeds on insect eggs and larvae, with beetle larvae being its favourite.

Animals of the Great Victoria Desert

Hundreds of animal species live in this sand desert – each adapted to its harsh conditions. Marsupials (mammals with pouches) and reptiles are well suited to the heat, alongside a wide variety of birds, rodents, and other mammals. New species are still being discovered, especially in the large desert areas protected as nature reserves.

The bandy-bandy is famous for its alternating black and white bands.

Bandy-bandy
(Vermicella annulata)

The bandy-bandy, or hoop snake, spends the day in its burrow and hunts at night, killing prey with a venomous bite. When threatened, it uses an unusual defense to appear more menacing – twisting its body into tall loops, while keeping the head and tail on the ground.

Summer sleep

During dry conditions, the water-holding frog stays underground and enters a period known as summer sleep, or aestivation. This is when the frog becomes inactive and survives on water stored in its bladder or pockets under its skin. The frog also lines its burrow with old skin to keep it waterproof. It can stay like this for years until the rain comes again.

Great desert skink
(Egernia kintorei)

These lizards live with their families in large burrows in the sand dunes. They work together to dig and maintain the burrows, which can extend up to 12 m (40 ft) in length. The skinks make as many as 20 entrances to the burrows and keep a separate area where they poop.

Sandhill dunnart
(Sminthopsis psammophila)

The dunnart is a small marsupial. It has beady, black eyes and a tail almost as long as its body. It sleeps during the day in a nest under a log or rock. At night, the dunnart comes out to hunt insects, spiders, and small reptiles.

The male mallee fowl uses its powerful legs to dig a pit in the sand.

Mallee fowl
(Leipoa ocellata)

To make a nest, the male mallee fowl first digs a hole in the sand. Then, the bird fills it with leaves and twigs until it becomes a large mound. The female lays her eggs in a dip on top, which is later covered with more sand and leaves.

HOT AND DRY DESERTS

Desert devil

Despite its name, the thorny devil is not fierce at all. It feeds on ants – waiting for a trail to pass by before licking them up with its short, sticky tongue. Being active during the day puts the desert devil at greater risk of being spotted by predators. So, along with its fearsome-looking spines, it has a bizarre, rocking way of walking with its tail held up, to confuse enemies into leaving it alone.

Colours

Brilliantly camouflaged in grey and brown, the thorny devil can change colour to yellow, orange, or red to match its surroundings more closely. It is paler in summer and turns darker in the colder, winter months, or when it is alarmed.

GREAT VICTORIA DESERT

False head

Most of the thorny devil's body is covered in sharp triangular spines that help warn off predators. It also has a spiny "false head" on the back of its neck. By lowering the actual head, it tricks enemies into attacking the less important false head instead.

The thorny devil can grow up to 21 cm (8 in) in length.

Water catcher

The thorny devil has a unique way of collecting water. It rubs against plants covered in morning dew, trapping moisture in the grooves between its scales. Tiny tubes beneath the scales then carry the water across its body, all the way to its mouth.

HOT AND DRY DESERTS

Ooldea mallee
(Eucalyptus youngiana)

This bush-like gum tree is best known for its eye-catching flowers. Brilliant red, pink, or yellow blooms burst from large, cone-shaped buds, arranged in sets of three on the branches. They appear from June to October during the Australian winter.

River red gum tree
(Eucalyptus camaldulensis)

A river red gum tree can grow up to 45 m (150 ft) tall. Thanks to its many survival skills, it can live for more than 500 years. Since seedlings are easily damaged by the heat, these trees drop their leaves to save water and grow new ones when it rains.

Plants of the Great Victoria Desert

While the Great Victoria Desert is hot and dry, it is full of life. Large, open woodlands of gum trees are dotted with hummocks of spinifex and other grasses. Salt bush and bluebush are among plants that can tolerate high levels of salt and grow well near salt lakes. Meanwhile, gibber plains may come alive with wildflowers after heavy rain.

Desert in bloom

After a heavy downpour, the dry landscape of the Great Victoria is suddenly blanketed in a colourful carpet of wildflowers. Blooming almost overnight, they emerge from seeds that may have spent years in the ground, quickly taking advantage of the rain to sprout.

Spinifex grass
(Triodia basedowii)
Clumps of this silvery-green grass grow all over the Great Victoria. Nicknamed "porcupine grass", its long leaves have sharp tips that can break off on contact with skin. A vital food source for many desert animals, it also plays an important role in stabilizing sand dunes.

Common mulga tree
(Acacia aneura)
In the Great Victoria Desert, mulgas rise as small, hardy trees with spikes of bright yellow flowers. Instead of leaves, they have thin, flat needles covered in fine silver hairs. The leaves are cleverly arranged to funnel water towards the trunk and roots, helping the mulgas survive long droughts.

Silver emu bush
(Eremophila scoparia)
Silver emu bushes grow in sandy soil among mulga and mallee trees. They are well suited to their dry habitat as they require very little water to survive. The silver colour of their leaves helps reflect sunlight. In spring, they are covered in delicate tufts of pink, tube-like flowers.

Honeysuckle grevillea
(Grevillea juncifolia)
The honeysuckle grevillea flourishes among grass-covered sand dunes. It has fine, spiky leaves that grow up to 30 cm (12 in) long. The plant flaunts clusters of golden-yellow flowers, which produce large amounts of nectar to attract birds and insects.

It is also known as the honeysuckle spider flower, inspired by the spidery shape of its flowers.

Nullarbor Plain

To the south of the Great Victoria lies a massive limestone plain, edged with steep cliffs that drop into the ocean. It spans about 260,000 km^2 (100,400 miles^2). This is the Nullarbor Plain, named from the Latin for "no trees", and one of Australia's most famous landscapes. Largely covered in scrub and dotted with more than 250 caves, the Nullarbor harbours many rare animals, including bearded dragons and hairy-nosed wombats.

Coastal deserts

Coastal deserts are usually found along the western edges of continents. These include the Atacama in South America and the Namib in Africa. Despite lying so close to water, these deserts are among the driest places on Earth. This is because most of the moisture falls into the sea as rain before it can reach land. Winters are cool, summers are warm, and these sea-hugging areas are often cloaked in fog.

FACT FILE

Area
105,200 km² (40,600 miles²)

Average rainfall
Less than 15 mm (0.6 in)

Average temperature
−4 to 35°C (25 to 95°F)

Atacama Desert

In the world's driest desert outside the polar regions, some places have gone without rain for decades, making life very difficult.

A long, narrow desert, the Atacama hugs the coast of northern Chile. From the border with Peru in the north, it stretches for around 960 km (600 miles) south but is less than 160 km (100 miles) wide in most places. To the east, the foothills of the mighty Andes Mountains loom over the sun-scorched terrain.

Wildflowers paint the desert in shades of purple, yellow, and red.

Flowering desert

Some parts of the Atacama are so dry that no plants can grow. But on rare occasions when rain does fall, the seeds or bulbs that have lain underground for years suddenly sprout. Soon, the usually bare, parched desert is covered in wildflowers.

The Atacama coast

The Atacama Desert lies along the Pacific Ocean, the world's largest ocean. In some areas, it forms a narrow strip of rock and sand between the ocean and the mountains. In others, dramatic, reddish-brown cliffs plunge straight into the water.

SOUTH AMERICA

Pan de Azúcar

Blending two vastly different habitats, Pan de Azúcar is a one-of-a-kind national park. Desert wildlife, such as guanaco and cacti, live alongside ocean animals, including penguins and sea lions, all set against a stunning backdrop.

COASTAL DESERTS

Fog formation

Despite the lack of rainfall, the Atacama receives some moisture in the form of fog, known as "camanchaca". It forms along the Pacific coast, then moves inland as thick clouds. The fog is made up of tiny water droplets, which are so light that they do not fall as rain.

Camanchaca fog — Atacama Desert — Atlantic Ocean — Andes Mountains — Coastal Range — Humboldt Current (Cold ocean current) — Pacific Ocean

The branches of trees and bushes trap the fog.

Geography of the Atacama Desert

The Atacama Desert is a high plateau reaching up to 5,000 m (16,000 ft) above sea level. The terrain is mostly rocky or stony, with tall sand dunes, large salt lakes, and deep canyons. Nestled between the sea and mountains, the region stays dry. The Humboldt Current blocks rain clouds from the west and the mountains prevent moist air from the east.

Fog oasis

Even in this bare, parched desert, there are pockets of greenery. You will find isolated hills covered in vegetation, watered entirely by fog. These fog "oases" are locally known as "lomas", or hills, and are home to hundreds of different species of plants.

ATACAMA DESERT

Rocky landscape

This striking rock formation rises above the Salar de Tara, a huge salt flat in the Atacama. Formed from volcanic rock, it is known as the Cathedrals of Tara (Catedrales de Tara) because its pointed peaks resemble the soaring spires of a church.

Dry as a bone

Outside Antarctica, the Atacama is the driest place on Earth. Throughout the desert, the average rainfall is as low as 5 mm (0.2 in) a year, with some places experiencing almost no rain at all for centuries. In the desert heat, water that does fall evaporates quickly.

COASTAL DESERTS

Animals of the Atacama Desert

With its extreme water scarcity, the Atacama Desert is one of the harshest environments on Earth. Some parts of the desert are too dry for any plants and animals to survive. But other areas, such as fog oases in the mountains, salt flats, and coastal cliffs and islands, shelter remarkably hardy wildlife.

Guanaco
(Lama guanicoe)

The guanaco is one of the few mammals that can survive in the Atacama. A member of the camel family, the guanaco lives in small groups of females that are often headed by a male. They graze on cacti and lichens, which are watered by fog.

Darwin's leaf-eared mouse
(Phyllotis darwini)

Named after its leaf-shaped ears, this little mouse eats insects, berries, and seeds. Its eating habits play a significant role in desert life. Some seeds pass through the rodent's droppings, scatter, and grow into new plants, if the conditions are right.

The lizard uses its tail for balance as it leaps after flies.

Fabian's lizard
(Liolaemus fabiani)

In the severe conditions of a desert salt flat, only the toughest survive. The key to this lizard's survival is a diet of brine flies, which serves as both food and water. However, to get just a teaspoon of water, it must consume at least 400 flies.

ATACAMA DESERT

Mountain vizcacha
(Lagidium viscacia)

Vizcachas look like large rabbits, but with thicker fur and long, curly tails. Agile climbers, they live among rocks and crags, and have fleshy pads on their paws to help them grip. During the day, vizcachas feed on moss and grasses, then perch on a rock to rest or sunbathe.

Desert cliffs

Penguins are an unusual sight in a desert, but thousands of Humboldt penguins breed on rocky cliffs and islands along the Atacama coast. They are drawn here by the abundance of fish such as anchovies, brought by the passing waters of the Humboldt Current.

Large, pointed ears help the fox to listen out for prey.

South American gray fox
(Lycalopex griseus)

To avoid the searing heat of the day, the South American gray fox comes out only at dusk and dawn. Meals are scarce in the Atacama so the unfussy fox eats whatever it can find – plants or animals. It gets most of the water it needs from the food it eats.

COASTAL DESERTS

Andean flamingo

In the middle of the Atacama Desert lies a vast, shimmering salt lake. Called the Salar de Atacama, it is one of the most challenging habitats imaginable. Very few animals stand a chance here, but Andean flamingos have adapted to thrive in this environment that is too deadly for most living things.

Feeding

Andean flamingos mainly live on shrimps and algae. As they wade into the lake, they stir up the water with their long legs. This makes it easier for them to spot any food. Then, they stretch their long necks down, dip their heads and bills under, and start to feed.

Nesting

To build their nests, Andean flamingos scoop up mud with their bills and smooth it into a tall mound with their feet. The female lays a single egg in a dip on top. Both parents take turns to keep the egg warm until it hatches.

The parents care for the newly hatched chick in the early weeks.

Curved bill

An Andean flamingo's yellow-and-black curved bill is designed for filter feeding. It is lined with stiff, bristle-like plates that act like a sieve. With its head in the water, the flamingo sweeps its bill from side to side, filtering out tiny food items to eat.

ATACAMA DESERT

Pretty in pink

A flamingo's famous pink colour comes from pigments in the food it eats. But it does not start off like that – newly hatched chicks are grey or white. It can take up to 3 years for them to grow their fabulous adult feathers.

COASTAL DESERTS

Tamarugo
(Prosopis tamarugo)

This tough, bushy tree is able to grow well in the Atacama because it does not rely on rainfall. Instead, it has long roots for reaching water up to 12 m (40 ft) underground. This allows it to thrive even in the extreme environment of the desert's salt lakes.

White suspiro
(Nolana baccata)

After a rare shower of rain, the desert may be covered in a carpet of wildflowers. Among them are showy white blooms of the white suspiro plant. It shares its name with a fluffy white meringue treat – called suspiro – which is popular in South America.

Plants of the Atacama Desert

Parts of the Atacama are so dry that no plants are able to survive there. In other places, only plants that are highly adapted to the dry or salty soil stand any chance of staying alive. Along the coasts, conditions are more favourable. Here, the camanchaca fog rolling in from the ocean provides enough moisture for plants to grow, including cacti and thorny trees.

Desert lichens
(Roccellina portentosa)

Lichens like this one may look grey and dead, but they are actually a combination of algae and fungi. In the Atacama, they grow alongside cacti in fog oases, where the fog is their only source of moisture. Some grow on desert rocks while others take root on cacti spines and stems.

Llareta
(Azorella compacta)

Looking like a giant, green cushion, llareta grows on desert rocks high up in the mountains. The green is actually thousands of tiny leaves growing at the ends of the plant's stems. They fit so tightly together, you could sit on them and not fall through.

The plant has slender, green leaves.

The bright-coloured flowers attract insects for pollination.

Goat's horn
(Skytanthus acutus)

Goat's horn is a low, sprawling shrub that grows along the Atacama coast. Its tangled stems trap drifting sand and seeds, creating a mini-habitat for animals, especially lizards. It gets its name from its long, curly fruit, which looks like a goat's horns.

Copiapoa cacti
(Copiapoa spp)

Found only in the Atacama, these rare cacti grow in spiky clusters near the coast, where their sole source of moisture is the fog. The cacti grow very slowly – only around 1 cm (0.4 in) in a year – but they can reach the size of a small car.

Pussypaw
(Cistanthe longiscapa)

This plant bears gorgeous, deep pink flowers, each typically with five petals. It grows well in extremely dry places and is one of the many types of wildflower that burst into bloom after a rare downpour. Together, they create the famous "desierto florido", which means "blooming desert".

99

Valley of the Moon

A visit to this extraordinary valley in the Atacama Desert feels like being transported to the surface of the Moon. Its "lunar" landscape is a mix of sand dunes, salt lakes, mountains, and otherworldly rock formations, carved out by water and wind. A spectacular sight by day, the valley transforms at sunset, bathed in a magical glow of purples, pinks, and golds.

Namib Desert

FACT FILE

Area
160,000 km² (61,800 miles²)

Average rainfall
15 to 100 mm (0.6 to 4 in)

Average temperature
10 to 25°C (50 to 77°F)

A long, narrow strip along the Atlantic coast of Africa, the Namib may be the oldest desert in the world.

This cool, coastal desert stretches more than 2,000 km (1,250 miles) from Angola in the north to South Africa in the south, where it meets the Kalahari Desert. To the west, it borders the Atlantic Ocean and to the east lies a range of mountains called the Great Escarpment. Its average width is less than 160 km (100 miles).

Coastal dunes
Along the coast of Namibia, vast expanses of sand dunes meet the crashing waves of the Atlantic Ocean, creating a dramatic landscape. From the coast, the dunes reach inland, as far as the eye can see, shaped by the force of the wind.

The wind keeps the dunes in almost constant motion.

Fairy rings

Scattered about the Namib are mysterious, bare patches of sand surrounded by circles of grass. Local people believe that these "fairy rings" are footprints left by the gods. Some scientists think that they are made by termites, as a way of drawing water from the ground.

IN THE LOCAL LANGUAGE, "NAMIB" MEANS "A PLACE WHERE THERE IS NOTHING".

From rock to reservoir

Sesriem Canyon was carved out of desert rock over millions of years by the Tsauchab River. Today, the river is usually dry but quickly turns into a torrent after heavy rain. Whenever this happens, the canyon becomes a vital source of water for desert animals.

AFRICA

COASTAL DESERTS

Geography of the Namib Desert

The Namib is estimated to be about 55 million years old, possibly making it the world's oldest desert. It sits on a huge platform of rock that slopes gradually from the Atlantic coast to the base of the mountains. In the south, the rock is covered in vast stretches of sand. Scattered mountains and gravel plains lie in the north.

Great barrier

The steep cliffs of the Great Escarpment run along the southern edge of Africa – from Angola in the north, through Namibia, and down into Mozambique. These cliffs act like a barrier between the wetter regions inland and the dry desert along the coast.

NAMIB DESERT

Climate

The Namib is scorching hot during the day, but temperatures can drop below freezing at night. It receives very little rainfall – some years, none at all. Along the coast, fog rolls in from the sea for about 180 days. This occurs when cold air from the ocean current meets hot air from inland.

Lagoons

Several large lagoons, such as Walvis Bay, lie along the coast. They are formed when sand spits – narrow bodies of sand – extend across a bay, closing it off from the open sea. The shallow lake of water behind becomes a lagoon. Thousands of birds flock here to breed and feed.

Desert giants

Sossusvlei is a dry lakebed surrounded by deep-orange sand dunes that rise hundreds of metres into the air. The sand gets its colour from iron oxide – the brighter the colour, the older the dune. Among these towering dunes stand dead acacia trees, some over a thousand years old.

COASTAL DESERTS

Gemsbok
(Oryx gazella)

Gemsbok have a special system of blood vessels and nasal tubes that cools blood before it reaches their brains. Able to go for days without a drink, they get water from water holes and plants, as well as by digging into underground reserves.

Dune ant
(Camponotus detritus)

This large ant lives in colonies in the dunes, where it builds its nest among the roots of plants. It forages for insects during the hottest part of the day. The fine, silver hairs on its striped abdomen reflect sunlight, helping the ant keep cool.

Animals of the Namib Desert

The arid landscape of the Namib hosts an astonishing number of animals. The ever-changing dunes provide habitats for insects, rodents, and reptiles. Birds, jackals, and seals live along the shore, while elephants and rhinos roam the gravel plains. Many of these creatures depend on fog for water, which condenses as water droplets on the sand, rocks, and even their own bodies.

Ostrich
(Struthio camelus)

Although they can't fly, ostriches are the fastest birds on land, sprinting at over 70 kph (45 mph). To stay warm, they cover the skin on their legs and sides with their wings. To cool down, they leave their skin bare.

Grant's golden mole
(Eremitalpa granti)

Although it lives among the sand dunes, the golden mole finds it impossible to dig tunnels in the loose, shifting sand. Instead it "paddles" through the dunes using its broad claws, searching for lizards, crickets, and beetle grubs to eat.

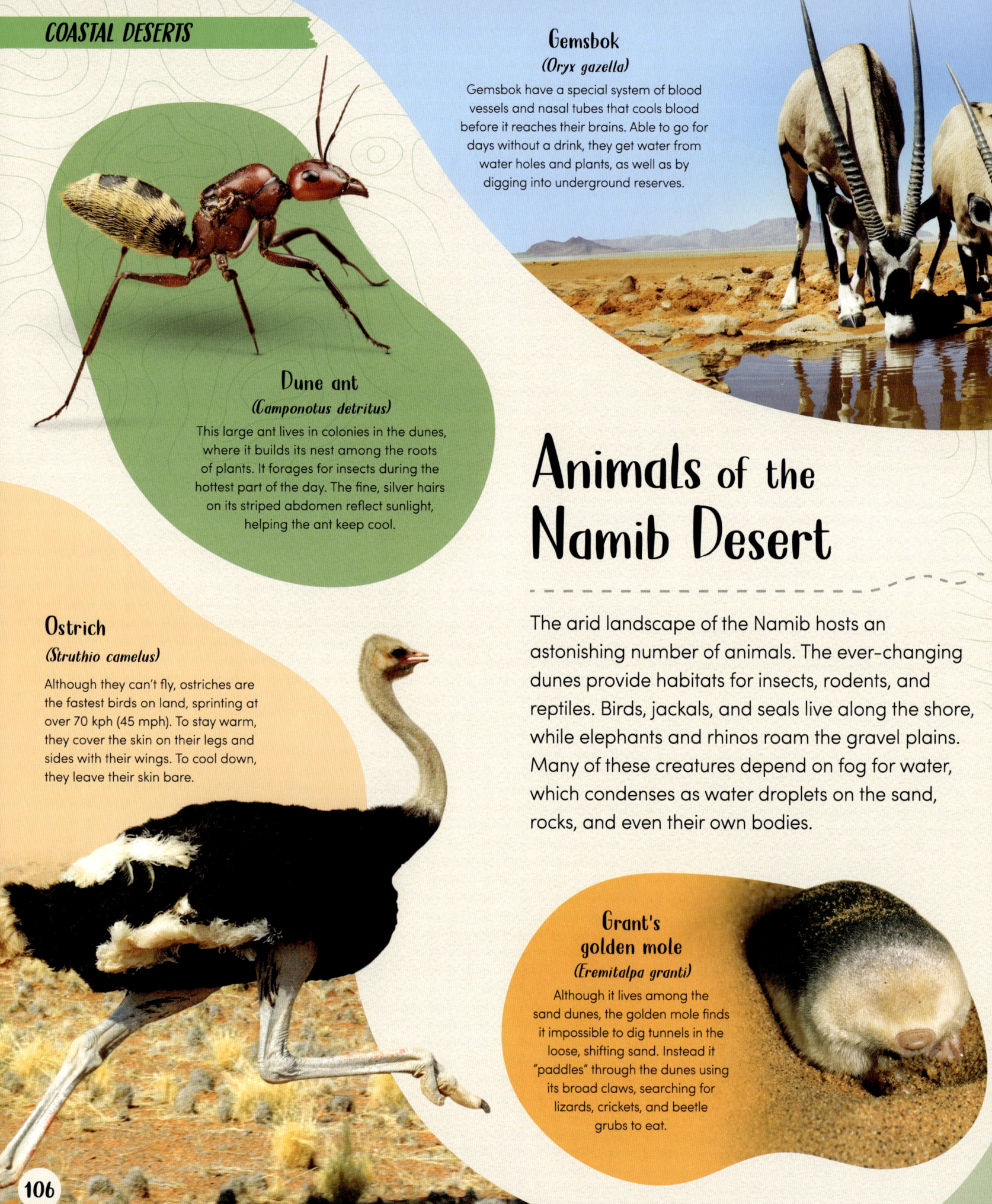

Golden wheel spider
(Carparachne aureoflava)

If a golden wheel spider wants to escape from a predatory wasp, it buries itself in a silk-lined burrow in the sand. If it cannot make it into the burrow, it flips on to its side and cartwheels down the dune at high speed, out of harm's way.

Drinking fog

In the early morning hours, the Namib Desert beetle climbs to the top of a dune, lifts its back into the air, spreads its wings, and basks in the incoming fog. It waits as the water droplets from the fog collect on tiny bumps on its body and trickle down to its mouth. Then, the beetle hurriedly burrows into the sand to shield itself from the searing heat.

Its ears can grow up to 2 m (6 ft) long and 1 m (3 ft) wide.

African bush elephant
(Loxodonta africana)

African elephants are usually at home on grassland, but they have also learned to live in the desert. Their long legs and large feet make it easy for them to walk on sand. But more importantly, they can go for several days without drinking while searching for the next water hole.

COASTAL DESERTS

Plants of the Namib Desert

The Namib Desert is so old that many unique plants can be found there. Near the coast, algae and lichens get water from the fog. Bushes and tall grasses grow among the sand dunes. When it rains, the bare parts of the desert quickly fill with short grasses. Nearby, there are also plants that look like smooth pebbles or spiky melons, and some that grow only two leaves in their entire lifetime.

Dune grass
(Stipagrostis sabulicola)

Thanks to its special roots, this tough grass can grow in thick mounds on dunes in the driest parts of the Namib. Its roots lie just above or close to the surface of the sand, spreading out over many metres to absorb moisture from fog, dew, or rain.

Hoodia
(Hoodia currorii)

This strange-looking desert succulent produces cap-shaped, rusty-red flowers at the ends of its tall, spiky stems. The flowers are covered in purple hairs and can grow as big as an adult human hand. They give off a terrible smell, like rotting meat, which attracts insect pollinators, such as flies.

Nara plant
(Acanthosicyos horridus)

Found only in the Namib, this sprawling plant grows on the lower slopes of sand dunes. It has long, thick roots for reaching water under the surface, and stems and spines instead of leaves. Its prickly, melon-shaped fruit are eaten by many desert animals.

NAMIB DESERT

Blowing in the wind

In the Namib, 120 different species of lichen grow on or even inside rocks. Some, like the *Xanthomaculina convulata*, are not attached to any surface. Carried by the wind, they can grow wherever they land, allowing them to colonize, or take over, new areas of the desert.

Pencil bush
(Arthraerua leubnitziae)

The hardy pencil bush grows along the coast, where it gets water and nutrients from the fog. It has rectangular leaves and white flowers, which provide food for small desert rodents. It also offers safe homes to some animals, including desert mice, who build their nests among its stems.

Quiver tree
(Aloidendron dichotomum)

With thick trunks and long, forked branches, these plants look like trees, but are actually succulents. Their trunks are modified stems that hold water. They also store water in their spiky leaves, which grow in rosettes at the tips of the branches.

Lithops
(Lithops francisci)

Also called "pebble plants", lithops form clusters of thick, fleshy, grey-green leaves that look just like stones. On the slopes where they grow, they are brilliantly camouflaged against the rocks. This protects them from animals who like to munch on their leaves.

109

COASTAL DESERTS

Leaves

Tumboa leaves grow very slowly but can reach 6–9 m (20–30 ft) in length. They sprawl across the ground, soaking up water from the fog. As they grow, the leaves are blasted by the wind and chewed by animals, ending up shredded into long, dry-looking strands.

Cones

New tumboa plants grow from cones instead of flowers. They rely on insects, such as wasps and flies, to carry pollen from male to female cones, so seeds can form. A medium-sized plant can produce more than 10,000 seeds, which may be carried away by the wind.

Tumboa

In the Namib, about 50 km (31 miles) away from the coast, lies a sunbaked plain covered in sand and gravel. Scattered across it are one of the most unusual plants in the world – *Welwitschia mirabilis*. Known locally as "tumboa", these plants grow low to the ground, and have wide, woody stems and long roots. They can live for hundreds or even thousands of years. The plants produce only two leathery leaves that last their entire lifespan – a unique feat for a plant.

NAMIB DESERT

Roots

Tumboa plants have very long, thick main roots that can reach as deep as 1.5 m (5 ft) or more underground to access water. As they grow downwards, they split into many side roots. The roots take in moisture from the fog that has turned into drops on the leaves and been absorbed by the soil.

Skeleton Coast

At the northern end of the Namib Desert sits the Skeleton Coast. Originally named after the many whale bones that washed ashore, it is also famous for shipwrecks. Over the years, hundreds of ships have run aground in the thick fog that shrouds the coastline. Some wrecks have been swallowed by the shifting sands. Others can still be seen, rusting on the ground.

Cold winter deserts

With long, warm summers and short, cold winters, these deserts live up to their name. They are also extremely dry, as they lie next to high mountain ranges that block moisture from reaching them. Two of the world's most notable cold winter deserts include the Gobi in Asia and the Great Basin in North America. Both are dry and windswept, yet strikingly different in appearance. The Gobi is vast and rugged, stretching across parts of China and Mongolia. The Great Basin, on the other hand, is higher in elevation, with mountain ranges and broad, open valleys.

FACT FILE

Area
1.3 million km² (500,000 miles²)

Average rainfall
10 to 250 mm (0.4 to 10 in)

Average temperature
−40 to 45°C (−40 to 113°F)

Gobi Desert

Lying south of the Altai and Hangayn Mountains, the Gobi covers an area larger than Germany and France combined.

The largest desert in Asia, the Gobi lies across southern Mongolia and northern China. It is bordered by mountains to the north, south, and east. Much of the Gobi's landscape is bare rock, with only a small portion made of sand dunes. A place of extreme temperatures, the difference between a scorching summer's day and a freezing winter's night in the Gobi can be as much as 53°C (127°F).

Kulan can run at speeds of up to 64 kph (40 mph).

Kulan

Also known as Mongolian wild asses, kulan live in herds in the Gobi. They are constantly on the move, travelling long distances across the desert in search of water and plants. It is believed that they cover a distance of 70,000 km² (27,000 miles²) every year.

THE FAMOUS SILK ROAD ONCE WENT THROUGH THE GOBI DESERT.

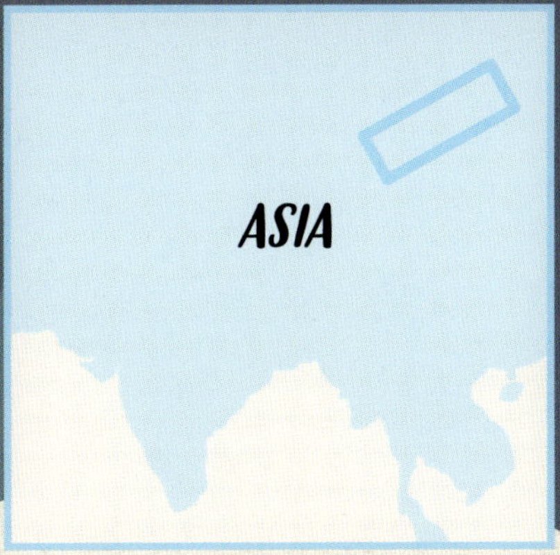

ASIA

Sandy sounds

The imposing Khongor sand dunes rise hundreds of metres into the air. They are also called the "Singing Sands" because of the high-pitched noise made when the wind blows over the sand. Some people think that it sounds like an aircraft taking off.

Parched land

A vast, rocky plain, the Trans-Altai Gobi is the driest part of the Gobi Desert. It receives less than 100 mm (4 in) of rain every year, leaving the ground parched and cracked. For the animals found here, such as wild camels and Gobi bears, life is a constant battle to survive.

117

COLD WINTER DESERTS

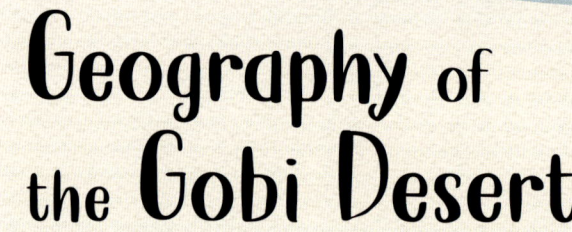

Desert rocks
The Gobi is mostly made up of rocks, such as basalt and granite, formed by ancient volcanic eruptions. The region also contains limestone and sandstone, made from sediments left behind by ancient rivers, lakes, and seas. Many exciting fossil discoveries have been found in these sedimentary rocks.

Cold climate
Apart from Antarctica, the Gobi is the world's coldest desert, with winter temperatures plummeting to −40°C (−40°F). Summers, in contrast, are scorching hot, reaching as high as 45°C (113°F). They are also extremely dry, receiving less than 70 mm (3 in) rain in a year.

Geography of the Gobi Desert

Unlike many deserts, very little of the Gobi is covered in sand. Instead, its landscape ranges from high mountains and rounded hills to wide valleys, dry riverbeds, and rocky plains. The centre of the desert is mostly "desert pavement", where layers of gravel lie on top of stony soil. Apart from a scattering of salt marshes, there is hardly any water around.

Mesa is named after the Spanish word for "table" because of its flat top.

Mesa

Butte is a French word that means "knoll" or "hill".

Butte

Mesas and buttes
Among the many dramatic rock features of the Gobi landscape are mesas and buttes. Both are flat-topped, steep-sided hills, but mesas are generally wider and shorter than buttes. They are formed as wind and water erode the softer layers of surrounding rock.

Mountain wall

The Gobi is surrounded on three sides by towering peaks, including the Altai Mountains shown here. These mountains block nearly all the moisture carried by winds blowing into the desert. This "rain-shadow" effect is one of the major reasons why the desert is so dry.

COLD WINTER DESERTS

Animals of the Gobi Desert

Alongside some rare animals, such as kulan and wild Bactrian camels, the Gobi supports a surprising variety of mammals, reptiles, and birds. The most common mammals are jerboas and gerbils, while birds include sandgrouse, vultures, and eagles. Grasshoppers and beetles feed on the sparse desert plants, and lizards scurry across the sand. All are remarkably adapted to survive in this harsh terrain.

Long-eared hedgehog
(Hemiechinus auritus)

The most striking feature of this hedgehog is its long, furry ears. They help radiate heat to keep the animal cool. During the day, it stays hidden in a burrow and comes out at night to hunt for lizards and insects. It uses its excellent hearing and sense of smell to locate prey.

Hairy-footed jerboa
(Dipus sagitta)

With back legs twice as long as their front legs, these small mammals are built for hopping. As they leap forward, they use their long, whip-like tails for balance. Fine hairs on their feet give them extra grip when landing on loose sand.

Last of their kind

The Gobi bear is the only bear species that can withstand the tough desert conditions. It's also one of the rarest animals on Earth, with as few as 40 left in the wild. Among the many threats it faces are climate change, habitat loss, and scarcity of food.

GOBI DESERT

Golden eagle
(Aquila chrysaetos)

Flying high above the desert, a golden eagle is an amazing sight. To save energy as it flies, this bird of prey rides rising columns of air, called thermals. Once it spots a hare or marmot with its exceptional vision, the eagle swoops down and grabs the prey with its sharp talons.

With broad, powerful wings, the bird soars and glides across the desert sky.

Gobi pit viper
(Gloydius stejnegeri)

This venomous desert snake hunts at night, when the temperature drops. It locates prey, such as rodents, in the dark using special sense organs. Positioned between the snake's eyes and nostrils, these organs detect heat given off by the warm-blooded prey.

Kulan
(Equus hemionus)

An expert digger, the kulan plays a vital role in the desert ecosystem. To reach underground water, it uses its front hooves to dig holes in dry riverbeds. These life-saving "watering holes" are then used by other desert animals to drink water.

Wild Bactrian camel
(Camelus ferus)

The famous two-humped Bactrian camel of the Gobi is now hard to find, with only around 950 left in the wild. Perfectly suited to desert life, the camel can survive for long periods without water. It can even drink water that is too salty for other animals.

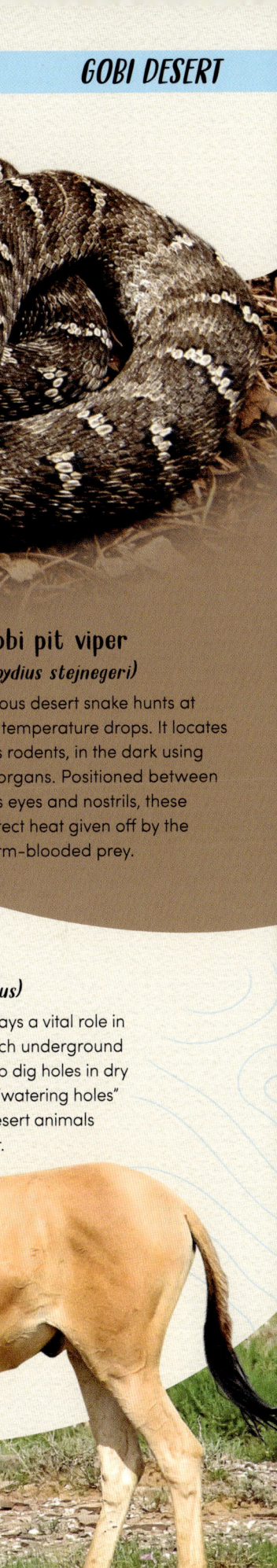

COLD WINTER DESERTS

Pallas's cat

About the size of a house cat, the Pallas's cat appears much larger thanks to its thick, furry coat. Mostly active at dawn and dusk, this elusive creature lives high up on the mountain slopes of the Gobi. It often hides behind rocks, repeatedly poking its head out to track prey, such as small rodents, lizards, and birds.

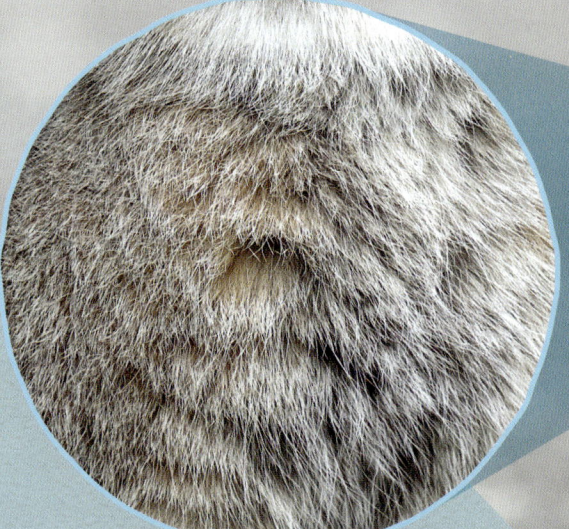

Fur

This cat's long, thick fur is essential to keep it warm in the freezing-cold mountains. Its silvery-grey coat, with shades of yellow or red, provides the perfect camouflage against the bare, rocky terrain of its home.

Ears

Adapted to withstand the cold, the cat's ears are small, flat, and set low on the sides of its head. Like the rest of its body, they're covered in thick fur for extra warmth.

Paws

Broad, fur-covered paws act like snowshoes, allowing it to move easily across frozen ground. The size and shape of the paws distribute the cat's weight more evenly, preventing it from sinking into the snow.

Tail

The cat has a long, silvery tail with black rings, about half the length of its body. It wraps its bushy tail around itself like a fluffy blanket. It's even been known to stand on its tail to keep its paws warm.

COLD WINTER DESERTS

In summer, bunches of small, bell-shaped flowers appear at the ends of the stems.

Spiny peashrub
(Caragana spinosa)

One of the toughest desert plants of all, the spiny peashrub can withstand extreme heat and cold, as well as drought and poor, salty soil. This spindly shrub grows along mountain rivers and streams in the Gobi, offering shelter to many animals.

Plants of the Gobi Desert

In many parts of the Gobi, the surface is covered in salt, left behind as water evaporates in the heat. Salt can damage and even kill plants, so vegetation is sparse. A few trees like tamarisk manage to grow near rivers or in places where groundwater is accessible. In sandy or gravelly areas, only the sturdiest grasses and shrubs survive. But salt isn't the only challenge – these plants must also endure extreme temperatures, fierce winds, and dry spells.

Mongolian chive
(Allium mongolicum)

Also called the "desert onion", this plant has strong stems and can reach a height of up to 20 cm (8 in). Long roots anchor it firmly to the ground, allowing the plant to access water deep below the surface. The roots also help bind the dry soil together, preventing the plant from being blown away by the wind.

Salt cedar
(Tamarix ramosissima)

Usually found in salty soil along riverbeds, this small tree has reddish branches with long, feathery blooms of pink flowers. To deter animals from eating its tiny green leaves, the plant pushes excess salt into the leaves, making them taste revolting.

Saltwort
(Salsola passerina)

Saltwort is one of the few species that can thrive in the harsh, salty desert. New plants grow when branches break off the main plant and are blown away by the wind, scattering seeds as they go.

The plant's small, grey-green leaves help minimize water loss.

Pamirian winterfat
(Krascheninnikovia ceratoides)

Growing up to 1 m (3 ft) tall, this desert shrub appears white due to a thick layer of silvery hairs covering its leaves. These help it survive both hot and cold conditions by reflecting sunlight and preventing damage from frost. The plant can also shed its leaves when water is scarce.

Storing water

Saxaul trees grow across the Gobi on gravel plains and rocky outcrops. They store water in their spongy bark, making them a hardy desert plant. People and animals squeeze the bark to extract water, to stay hydrated in the hot, dry desert.

Nemegt Basin

The Nemegt Basin lies in the southern part of the Gobi Desert in Mongolia. Known locally as the "Valley of the Dragons", it is renowned for the incredible fossils discovered here, including enormous plant-eating dinosaurs and pterosaurs. The fossils date back to about 70 million years ago, when the region had a humid climate and was mostly covered in rivers, lakes, and forests.

Across the desert

If you look out across the Great Basin, you'll see hills densely covered with bushy shrubs. This is sagebrush and, in many places, it stretches as far as the eye can see. This sweeping expanse is why the Great Basin is also known as "The Sagebrush Desert".

Sagebrush

The sagebrush provides shelter to many animals, such as grouse, mule deer, jackrabbits, and spadefoot toads. These creatures rely on the sagebrush plants for food and protection from fierce desert winds.

Great Basin Desert

FACT FILE

Area
409,000 km² (158,000 miles²)

Average rainfall
Less than 250 mm (10 in)

Average temperature
4 to 32°C (39 to 90°F)

Sandwiched between towering mountain ranges, the Great Basin is the largest desert in the USA.

The desert spans several US states, including most of Nevada, half of Utah, and parts of Oregon, California, Idaho, and Wyoming. Flanked by the Sierra Nevada to the west and the Rocky Mountains to the east, it is a land of isolated mountain ranges, dry valleys, and dramatic contrasts. To the south, it meets the Mojave Desert, where the land becomes even drier.

Strong winds bend the trees into twisted shapes.

Twisted trees

For over 10,000 years, forests of juniper and pinyon pine trees have grown on the slopes of the Great Basin mountains. Today, however, they are under threat due to wildfires, climate change, and the spread of plants that don't naturally grow there, such as cheatgrass.

COLD WINTER DESERTS

Geography of the Great Basin Desert

Unlike a typical desert, the Great Basin has a rolling, basin-and-range landscape. It consists of wide valleys (basins) separated by long, narrow mountain ranges that run parallel to each other. These features were formed over millions of years by movements of the Earth's tectonic plates. In some places, blocks of crust sank to form the basins while in others, the crust was lifted or pushed up to form the ranges.

Highs and lows

The Great Basin has many small basins, running in between chains of mountains. While the wetter mountain slopes can support forests of conifers, the soil in the basins is usually dry and salty.

Basin (valley)   Range (mountains)

Cool climate

Since the Great Basin lies in the rain-shadow area of several mountain ranges, it is very dry. More than half of the precipitation it receives falls as heavy snow in winter. While the winters are cold, with long periods of freezing temperatures, summers in the Great Basin are very hot.

Dry lakes

Dotted around the Great Basin are large, flat, dry lakebeds called playas. These lakebeds, such as the one at Black Rock Desert, are often found at the bottom of valleys. Here, water running off the mountains evaporates in the heat, leaving behind a bare, salty surface.

Rock glaciers slowly erode and shape mountains.

Desert glacier

You might not expect to see a glacier in a desert, so Wheeler Peak in the Great Basin will come as a surprise. This is a "rock glacier" – a landform consisting of a tongue-shaped mass of ice covered in broken pieces of rock, which moves slowly down the mountain slope.

Animals of the Great Basin Desert

From sagebrush seas and salt lakes to alpine forests filled with pinyon and juniper trees, the Great Basin has an amazing mix of animal habitats. Reptiles, such as gopher snakes and whiptail lizards, along with amphibians, like spadefoot toads, flourish here. There are also birds, including sage grouse and poorwill, and mammals, ranging from tiny kangaroo rats to prowling cougars.

Sage grouse
(Centrocercus urophasianus)
Sage grouse are large, turkey-like birds that live among the sagebrush, feeding on its leaves and seeds. To attract a mate, males puff up their necks, let their wings droop, and fan out their tails. Then, they strut about dramatically, hoping this display will woo a female.

Desert cottontail
(Sylvilagus audubonii)
Named after their white, cotton-like tails, these rabbits live among trees and shrubs. During the hottest part of the day, they shelter in dips in the ground or burrows left empty by other animals. When it cools down, they come out to nibble on grass, for food and water.

Great Basin rattlesnake
(Crotalus lutosus)
The rattlesnake sits and waits for a lizard or small mammal to pass by. When the animal is close, the snake makes its move and strikes. It kills its prey with venom injected through its long, sharp fangs. It also warns away predators, such as hawks and raptors, by rattling its tail.

This snake is usually light yellow, tan, or grey in colour.

GREAT BASIN DESERT

Burrow dwellers

Western burrowing owls do not dig their own nests. Instead, they use burrows abandoned by ground squirrels or marmots. Picking the right one is important. A burrow with a nearby perch is ideal, as it helps the owl watch for bobcats, coyotes, and other predators.

Townsend's big-eared bat
(Corynorhinus townsendii)

In winter, these medium-sized bats stay out of the cold by hibernating in a cave. Hanging upside down, they fluff up their greyish-brown fur and curl back their long ears. This prevents body heat from escaping and keeps them warm. The bats can stay like this for many months.

Piute ground squirrel
(Urocitellus mollis)

By hibernating in the winter and aestivating in the summer, this little squirrel escapes the worst of the desert heat and cold. It sleeps for around 8 months a year, waking up in spring and autumn to feed on desert grasses and seeds.

Cougar
(Puma concolor)

Cougars, or mountain lions, are top desert predators. They hunt elk and deer by stalking them and pouncing only when close enough. These powerful animals can drag prey three times their own weight. Often, they hide their kill under leaves or rocks and return to eat it later.

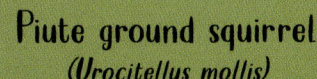

Cougars drink from desert streams, rivers, and lakes.

133

COLD WINTER DESERTS

Spadefoot toad

Dry deserts are difficult places for amphibians, since they need water to keep their skin moist for breathing and to lay their eggs. Yet the extraordinary spadefoot toad finds ways to survive in the Great Basin. While it can tolerate high levels of water loss, it spends much of its life underground in a burrow to avoid drying out in the hot sun. It can remain buried like this for months at a time.

The spades are made of keratin—the same material as your nails.

Skin

They are green or grey, with paler sides and bellies. Their skin is smoother than that of most other toads, and is dotted with tiny reddish-brown bumps. The toads release toxic chemicals from their skin to put off predators like rattlesnakes.

Spades

The toad gets its name from the hard, black ridges on the insides of its back feet, which it uses like spades for digging. By going backwards and moving its back feet in circles, a toad can bury itself very quickly in loose desert soil.

Tadpoles

After heavy rains, spadefoot toads breed quickly. They lay 300–500 tiny eggs in whatever water they can find – in shallow puddles, pools, or streams. The tadpoles hatch in just a few days, though it can take longer if the water is too cold.

Eyes

This toad has large, yellow eyes, set near the top of its head. Unlike most other toads that have horizontal pupils, its eyes have vertical, slit-like pupils. This helps the spadefoot toad see at night when it hunts for insects and spiders.

Its pupils are elongated in bright daylight and round in the dark.

COLD WINTER DESERTS

The tree gets its name from the prickly bristles that grow on its scaly cones.

Four-winged saltbush
(Atriplex canescens)

Saltbush is well adapted to salty places, such as playas. It gets rid of harmful salt through tiny hairs on its leaves. Its golden-yellow fruit have four papery "wings" and contain seeds inside. The wings catch the wind, carrying the fruit away to scatter their seeds.

Plants of the Great Basin Desert

More than 800 species of super-tough plants grow in the valleys and mountains of the Great Basin. Plants adapted to dry or salty conditions are usually found lower down, while those that need more water tend to grow higher up the slopes. The desert is best known for its vast expanses of sagebrush, but other plants, such as saltbush, greasewood, juniper trees, and bristlecone pines, are also a common sight.

Bristlecone pine
(Pinus longaeva)

The bristlecone pine is found only in the Great Basin, where it lives on rocky slopes. It is the longest-living tree in the world, capable of surviving for more than 4,000 years. Growing very slowly, it can endure harsher conditions than most other desert trees.

Green rabbitbrush
(Chrysothamnus viscidiflorus)

This low-growing shrub thrives among clumps of sagebrush and can spread quickly. It has short stems and thin, rectangular leaves that are often twisted or curled. In summer, the plant looks resplendent with bright yellow flowers, which is why it's also called the yellow rabbitbrush.

A sea of sagebrush

Almost half of the Great Basin is covered in sagebrush. A vital habitat for wildlife, sagebrush has small, grey-green leaves. Its roots are covered in fine hairs that help reduce water loss. These roots spread out for many metres around the trunks to absorb as much water as possible.

Instead of leaves, Utah junipers have short, stiff needles that help reduce water loss.

Black greasewood
(Sarcobatus vermiculatus)

Black greasewood is a fast-growing desert plant with black bark, spiny stems, and bright green, fleshy leaves. In summer, it flaunts spikes of small pink flowers at the tips of its stems. While it flourishes in dry conditions, it can also withstand flooding after heavy rain.

Utah juniper
(Juniperus osteosperma)

Utah juniper trees grow alongside pinyon pines and sagebrush on lower mountain slopes. In some places, they appear to grow straight out of the rock. Their secret to survival is a massive underground root system, which makes up about two-thirds of each tree.

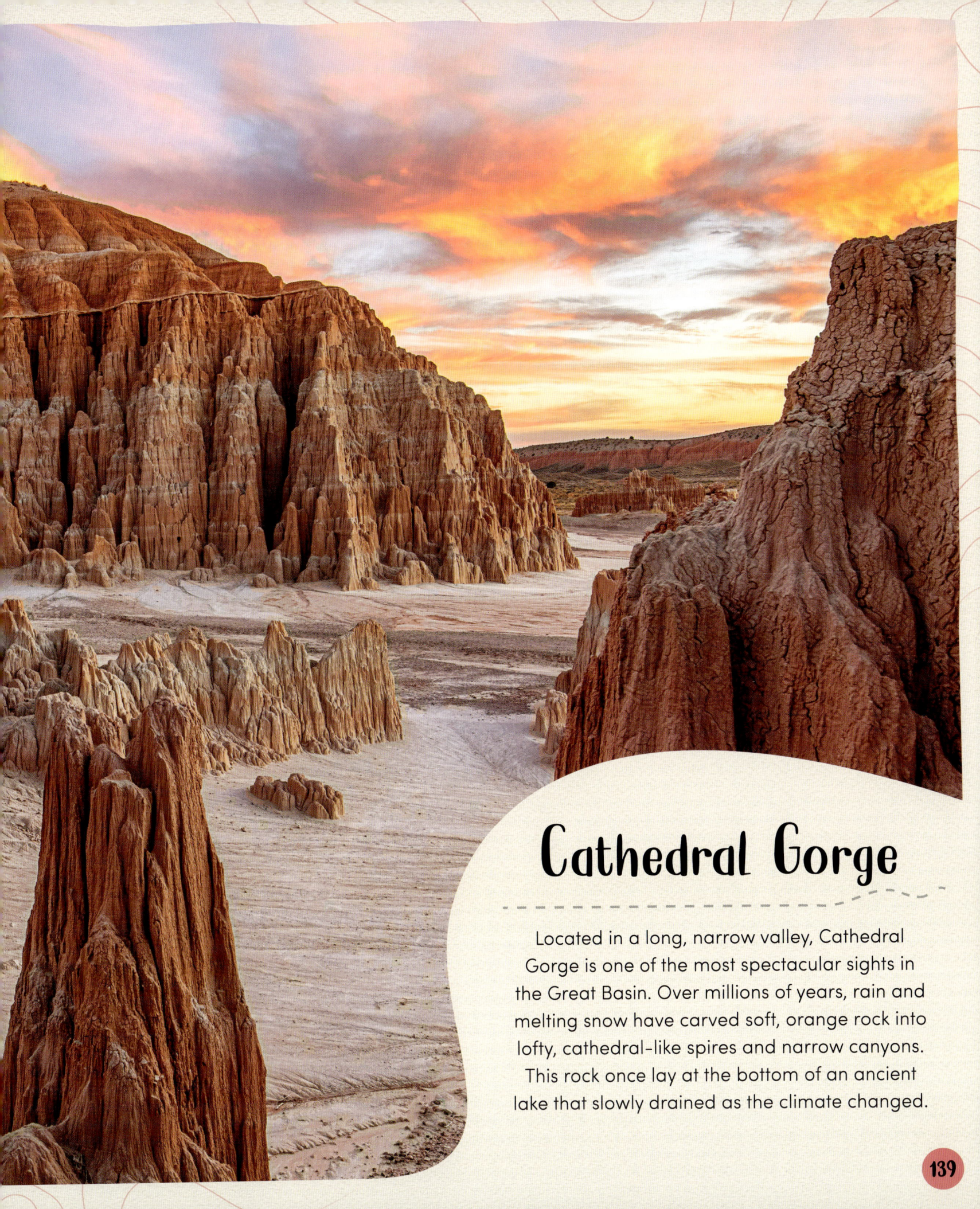

Cathedral Gorge

Located in a long, narrow valley, Cathedral Gorge is one of the most spectacular sights in the Great Basin. Over millions of years, rain and melting snow have carved soft, orange rock into lofty, cathedral-like spires and narrow canyons. This rock once lay at the bottom of an ancient lake that slowly drained as the climate changed.

Polar deserts

You need to head to the ends of the Earth to explore polar deserts – the Arctic in the north and Antarctica in the south. Both regions are freezing cold and covered in snow, but are considered deserts because they are extremely dry, receiving very little rain or snow. Antarctica is the world's largest polar desert. In fact, polar desert covers most of this vast, icy continent and only a few special plants and animals can live there.

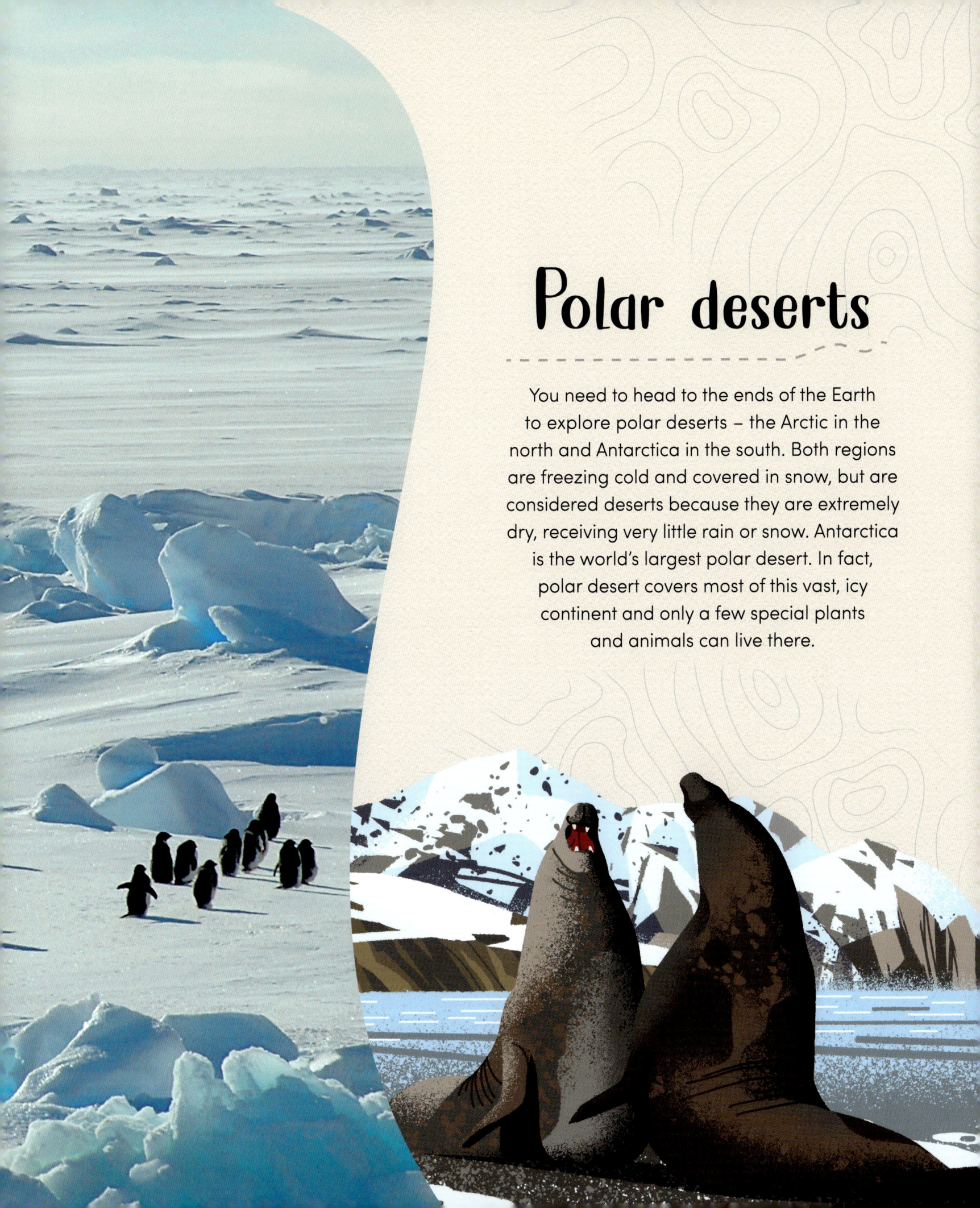

FACT FILE

Area
14.2 million km² (5.5 million miles²)

Average rainfall
166 mm (6.5 in)

Average temperature
−89 to 18°C (−130 to 65°F)

Antarctica

Along with being the coldest, highest, and windiest continent on Earth, Antarctica is also the driest of them all.

Antarctica is the fifth-largest continent in the world. It is larger than Oceania and Europe, and lies in the southernmost part of the planet. A vast ice sheet, more than 4.5 km (3 miles) thick in places, covers most of the land. In winter, the ice grows dramatically in size, as the Southern Ocean around Antarctica freezes over.

Male seals make loud, roaring sounds using their large, trunk-like noses.

Southern elephant seal

Some of the islands around Antarctica are home to southern elephant seals – the largest seals on the planet. These extraordinary animals are massive, with males weighing up to 4 tonnes (4.4 tons) and reaching 4.5 m (15 ft) in length.

Mount Erebus

More than 100 volcanoes lie hidden beneath the Antarctic ice. Two are still active – Deception Island and Mount Erebus on Ross Island. Famous for the lava lake in its crater, Mount Erebus has been erupting almost continuously for the past 60 years.

ANTARCTICA

Icy sheet

The Antarctic ice sheet forms the largest extent of ice on Earth. Around 60 per cent of the world's total fresh water is locked up inside it. In places, the ice sheet is so heavy it has pushed the land underneath it below sea level.

POLAR DESERTS

Geography of Antarctica

Located near the South Pole, Antarctica is surrounded by the stormy Southern Ocean. It is divided into West and East Antarctica by the Transantarctic Mountains – a vast chain stretching more than 3,200 km (2,000 miles) across the continent, from the Weddell Sea to the Ross Sea. Much of Antarctica's coastline is fringed with enormous ice shelves.

Climate

In winter (April to September), the average temperature at the South Pole is –60°C (–76°F). Along the coast it is warmer, ranging from –10 to –30°C (14 to –22°F). Antarctica also holds the world record for the lowest temperature ever recorded at –89.2°C (–128.5°F).

Dry ice

Despite its thick ice cover, Antarctica is considered a desert because it is extremely dry. Less than 200 mm (8 in) of precipitation falls each year, mostly as snow. The intense cold prevents the snow from melting, allowing it to slowly build up into a massive ice sheet over millions of years.

ANTARCTICA

Nunataks

Nunataks are jagged mountain peaks that jut through the surface of the surrounding glacial ice. Fierce winds prevent ice and snow from collecting on their steep slopes, leaving bare rock. Only about 0.4 per cent of Antarctica is free of ice and snow.

Dry valleys

The driest parts of Antarctica are the McMurdo Dry Valleys. Formed from rocks and dirt left behind by ancient glaciers, they receive less than 100 mm (4 in) of precipitation every year. Unlike anywhere else on Earth, the harsh conditions make them ideal for testing equipment that's used on Mars.

Mountains block rain from reaching the valleys.

Mountains prevent ice from flowing down.

Any water quickly evaporates due to the strong winds.

POLAR DESERTS

Animals of Antarctica

With its freezing temperatures, howling winds, and icy terrain, Antarctica is one of the most hostile habitats on Earth. The largest animal able to survive on land is a tiny midge. In the seas around Antarctica, however, it is a different story. Nutrients carried in by ocean currents make the Southern Ocean rich in food, supporting an incredible number of creatures.

Wingless springtail
(Cryptopygus antarctica)

Smaller than a grain of rice, the wingless springtail is one of the very few Antarctic creatures adapted to live on land. It has special chemicals that work like antifreeze in its body, preventing it from freezing. This helps it survive in temperatures as low as –25°C (–13°F).

Krill
(Euphausia superba)

Krill are small, shrimp-like creatures that move in swarms across the surface of the Southern Ocean. Some swarms are so huge they can be seen from space. They eat tiny plants called phytoplankton. In turn, many sea animals eat krill, making them an important part of the ocean food chain.

Filter feeders

In spring, humpback and blue whales arrive in the Southern Ocean to feed on krill. Instead of teeth, they have bristly plates of baleen that hang down from their upper jaws and act like enormous sieves. They gulp in ocean water, then filter it out – keeping only the food.

A humpback whale can eat more than 1,000 kg (2,200 lb) of small fish and krill in a day.

Orca
(Orcinus orca)
Orcas are skilled hunters that often work together in groups, called packs or pods, to catch penguins or seals. They use clicks and calls to coordinate their movements, falling silent just before striking. Then, they grab their prey with their sharp, conical teeth, which are as long as an adult human's thumb.

Antarctic midge
(Belgica antarctica)
This tiny insect lives year-round on land in Antarctica. It grows to a maximum length of just 6 mm (0.2 in). Most midges can fly, but the Antarctic midge has no wings. This helps it avoid being blown away by strong polar winds.

A snow petrel has a black bill and small black eyes.

Snow petrel
(Pagodroma nivea)
Snow petrels are among vast numbers of seabirds that rely on the Southern Ocean for food. These stunning, snow-white birds fly low over the water, dipping down to catch fish and squid. At other times, flocks of petrels can be seen perching on the edges of icebergs.

Southern elephant seal
(Mirounga leonine)
These huge seals are strong, graceful swimmers. A thick layer of blubber, or fat, keeps them warm. They can dive to depths of about 1,000 m (3,300 ft) to find fish and squid to eat. The seals can hold their breath for 20 minutes at a time.

POLAR DESERTS

148

Champion divers

Emperor penguins are superb swimmers and excellent divers. Using their short wings as paddles, they can reach greater depths and stay underwater longer than any other bird. The deepest penguin dive ever recorded was an incredible 564 m (1,850 ft).

ANTARCTICA

Cool dad

While the female penguin heads out to sea to hunt for food, the male stays behind to take care of the egg. It keeps the egg warm during severe winters by balancing the egg on its feet and covering it with feathered skin. The father can go without food for months while guarding the egg.

Emperor penguin

Emperor penguins live in the freezing cold of Antarctica. They are the largest of all penguin species and spend their entire lives on and around the ice. The penguins make their homes, called rookeries, on "fast ice", which is sea ice connected to land. Thick layers of feathers and body fat help to keep them warm in the extreme cold.

Huddle up

In the freezing Antarctic winter, male emperor penguins huddle in big groups of up to 5,000 birds to stay warm. They keep moving so each penguin takes a turn on the colder, windy side of the huddle. This also helps protect their chicks from predators.

POLAR DESERTS

Phytoplankton

Phytoplankton are microscopic, single-celled marine plants that play a vital role in Antarctica. They form the first link in every food chain in the Southern Ocean. Whales, seals, penguins, and seabirds all depend on them, either directly or indirectly, for their survival.

Different species of phytoplankton float in the sea.

The plant's thin leaves are often rolled or folded.

Antarctic hair grass
(Deschampsia antarctica)

This is one of the only two flowering plants in Antarctica. Its hardy hair grass grows in thick tufts close to the ground, staying low to avoid the harsh winds. During summer, it makes most of the limited sunlight to photosynthesize and grow.

Plants of Antarctica

Since most of the Antarctic continent is covered in ice, there are very few places where plants can grow. Only two species of flowering plants exist and there are no trees or shrubs. In rare, ice-free regions along the coast – in the dry valleys and on islands – mosses, liverworts, lichens, and fungi manage to survive, all adapted to the continent's extreme conditions.

Antarctic moss
(Schistidium antarctici)

Dense clumps of greenish-brown moss cover island rocks and soil, where it relies on melting snow and ice for water. If it is too cold for this to happen, the moss can dry itself out almost completely, then rehydrate when moisture is available.

ANTARCTICA

Blue-green algae
(Cyanobacteria)
Despite their name, blue-green algae are actually bacteria – microscopic living things that can make their own food, like plants. Extremely tough, they grow on and even inside rocks in dry valleys, forming slimy, green mats.

Antarctic pearlwort
(Colobanthos quitensis)
The only other flowering plant in Antarctica, pearlwort forms light green cushions along rocky shores. It can survive freezing temperatures as low as −15°C (5°F) using natural antifreeze. To withstand dry conditions, pearlwort can store minute amounts of moisture in special cells.

Orange lichen
(Xanthoria mawsonii)
This bright-orange lichen grows on rocks around the coast. Often found near bird colonies, it relies on bird droppings for essential nutrients. Lichens are well adapted to extreme environments, where they grow very slowly in the harsh conditions.

Icebergs

With an ear-splitting crack, a giant chunk of ice breaks off from the Antarctic ice sheet. This is called "iceberg calving" – a common sight in the Southern Ocean. Icebergs vary greatly in size – from as small as a car to as large as a city – but only about one-fifth of each is visible above the surface. Once calved, the icebergs drift on ocean currents for months, even years, until they reach warmer waters and begin to melt.

Glossary

ABDOMEN
the rear section of an insect's body

ADAPT
when an animal or plant changes over time to become better suited to its habitat

AESTIVATE
when an animal slows its body processes down to save energy during hot, dry summer weather

ALGAE
simple, plant-like organisms that live in water and make their food by photosynthesis (also see *photosynthesis*)

ANTENNAE
pair of long, thin sense organs, located near the front of an insect's head. Also called feelers

ARID
land or climate with little or no rain

BACTERIA
microscopic, single-celled organisms. Many bacteria are helpful, but some cause diseases

BURROW
hole or tunnel dug by animals for shelter or protection

CALVING
when an iceberg breaks off the end of an ice sheet or glacier

CAMOUFLAGE
when a plant or an animal is coloured, patterned, or shaped to merge into its surroundings

CARNIVORE
an animal that eats other animals

CIRCULATORY SYSTEM
the system of organs, such as the heart and blood vessels, that carry blood around an animal's body

CLIMATE CHANGE
change in temperature and weather across the Earth that can be natural or caused by human activity

COLONY
large group of one species of animal or plant, whose members all live closely together

CONDENSATION
the process of a gas changing into a liquid

CRESCENT
curved shape that is wider in the middle and narrow or pointed at the ends

CRUST
cold, hard, outer rock layer of the Earth, where all known life exists

CURRENT
the movement of wind or water in a specific direction

DROUGHT
long periods when there is little or no rain

ECOSYSTEM
a community of living things and their environment. An ecosystem may be as small as a puddle of water or as large as a desert

ENVIRONMENT
the living and non-living surroundings in which an animal or plant lives

EROSION
the wearing away of rock by natural forces, such as water, wind, or ice

EVAPORATION
the process of a liquid changing into a gas

EVERGREEN
plant or tree that doesn't shed its leaves and remains green the entire year

EXTINCT
an animal or plant species that has died out forever

FAULT
a break in Earth's crust along which rock is displaced

FILTER FEEDING
when small animals in water are strained or sieved out by larger creatures, such as baleen whales and flamingos, before being eaten

FORAGE
when animals search for food in the wild

GLACIER
huge, thick sheet of ice moving very slowly, either down the side of a mountain or over an area of land. Glaciers help to shape and form the landscape

HABITAT
the natural home of plants and animals, such as a desert or rainforest

HABITAT LOSS
destruction or reduction of a natural habitat

HERBIVORE
an animal that eats only plants

HIBERNATION
period of inactivity that some animals go through in the winter

Glossary

INCUBATE
when a parent bird sits on its eggs to keep them warm so that they can develop and hatch

LARVAE
insects, such as moths, that have hatched from the egg but have not yet developed into adults

LIFESPAN
length of time for which an animal is alive

MIGRATION
movement of animals from one place to another to find better sites for feeding and breeding

NUTRIENT
substance, such as protein, fat, or a vitamin, needed to provide essential nourishment for growth and function of a living being

OXYGEN
a gas in the air that all living things need to survive

PENINSULA
strip of land that is surrounded by water on three of its sides

PHOTOSYNTHESIS
the process by which green plants use the Sun's energy to make food from water and carbon dioxide

PLATEAU
large area of high, flat land. Some mountains, such as Table Mountain in Cape Town, South Africa, have a plateau at the top

POLLINATOR
animals that carry pollen from one flower to another so that seeds can grow and produce new plants

PRECIPITATION
any liquid or frozen water, such as rain and snow, that falls to Earth from the atmosphere

PREDATOR
animal that hunts and eats other animals

PREY
animal that is hunted and eaten by other animals

PRICKLY
an object that is spiny or bristly

PUPA
an insect at the third stage of complete development – between larva and adult

RIDGE
raised portion of a surface

RUST
reddish-brown minerals that form on iron and steel when they come into contact with water and oxygen

SAND SPIT
sand deposits that form along coasts or lakes

SCAVENGE
to gather or search an area for something, particularly food

SEDIMENT
small fragments of rock, sand, or mud that settle in layers, usually underwater

SPECIES
a particular type of living thing, such as a fennec fox or a bactrian camel. Only members of the same species can breed together

STINGER
sharp organ of an animal, such as a bee or scorpion, used to inject venom

SUCCULENT
plants that store water in their fleshy stems and leaves

TALONS
sharp claws of a meat-eating bird, such as an eagle, falcon, or owl

TECTONIC PLATES
enormous slabs of rock that make up the Earth's crust

VENOMOUS
substance that may be deadly if injected by an animal or plant through a sting or fangs

WATER HOLE
pool of water where animals go to drink

Index

A
adaptation 17, 34
addax 28, 33
Africa 8–9
Ahaggar Mountains 30–31
Altai Mountains 119
altitude 42
Amargosa Canyon 41
amphibians 81, 134–135
animals
  Antarctica 146–149
  Arabian Desert 68–71
  Atacama Desert 94–97
  desert species 16, 17
  endangered 24–25
  Gobi Desert 120–123
  Great Basin Desert 132–135
  Great Victoria Desert 80–81
  Mojave Desert 44–45
  Namib Desert 106–107
  Sahara Desert 32–33
  Thar Desert 56–59
Antarctica 14–15, 18, 21, 141, 142–153
Arabian Desert 11, 64–75
Aravalli Hills 52, 55
Arctic 20, 141
Asia 10–11
Asir Mountains 67
Atacama Desert 7, 18, 20, 90–101

B
bajadas 43
barchan dunes 22
basin-and-range deserts 42, 130
birds 16, 32, 45, 48, 57–59, 68, 80–81, 95–97, 106, 121, 132–133, 147–149
birds of prey 16
bustards, great Indian 58–59
buttes 23, 118

C
cacti 17, 46
calving, iceberg 153
camels
  Bactrian 120–121
  dromedary 34–35
Cathedral Gorge 138–139
cats, Pallas's 122–123
cheetahs, Saharan 25
Chihuahuan Desert 5, 20
climate change 24, 29, 139
coastal deserts 18, 88–113
cold winter deserts 18, 114–137
Colorado Plateau 20
conservation 25
cool, staying 17
coyotes 16, 44

D
Death Valley 50–51
desert pavements 23, 79
desertification 24
Devil's Playground 41
dry lakes 131
dry valleys 15, 145
dunes, sand 22, 28, 29, 30, 52, 55, 60, 65, 74, 76, 78, 102, 117
dung beetles 64, 69
duststorms 38–39

E
ergs 65
erosion 22, 23, 25

F
fairy rings 103
fish 45
flamingos, Andean 96–97
flash floods 22, 42, 43, 66
flooding 24
fog 89, 92, 107, 112
food webs 17
fossils 118, 127
foxes, fennec 17, 33

G
gas 65
gazelles, Dama 25
gibber plains 23, 79
Gibson Desert 21
glaciers, rock 131
global warming 24
Gobi Desert 11, 18, 21, 115, 116–127
Gondwanaland 78
Great Basin Desert 5, 50, 115, 128–139
Great Escarpment 102, 104
Great Sandy Desert 13, 21
Great Victoria Desert 13, 21, 76–87
gum trees, river red 77, 84–85

INDEX

H, I
habitats, desert 16
harmattan 31
hot and dry deserts 18, 26–87
Humboldt Current 92, 95
ice sheets 142, 143, 144, 153
icebergs 152–153
insects 44, 56, 64, 69, 106–107, 147
inselbergs 54
invertebrates 32, 68–69, 107, 146

J, K
Joshua trees 48–49
Kalahari Desert 8, 21
Karakum Desert 21
Karoo Desert 8
Khejri trees 53, 60
Khongor sand dunes 117
kulan 116, 121
Kunlun Mountains 19
Kyzylkum Desert 21

L
lagoons 105
Lake Sambhar 62–63
landforms 22–23
lunette dunes 78

M
McMurdo Dry Valleys 15, 145
Mars 19, 145
mesas 23, 118
mirages 67
Mojave Desert 5, 20, 40–51
montane deserts 19
Mount Erebus 143
mushroom rocks 23

N, O
Namib Desert 8, 21, 102–113
Nemegt Basin 126–7
nocturnal animals 28
North America 4–5
Nullarbor Plain 86–87
nunataks 145
oases 31
  fog 92
Oceania 12–13
oil 65
oryx, Arabian 70–71

P
Pan de Azúcar 91
parabolic dunes 22, 55
Patagonian Desert 7, 20
penguins, emperor 148–149
plants
  Antarctica 150–151
  Arabian Desert 72–73
  Atacama Desert 90, 98–99
  desert species 16, 17
  Gobi Desert 124–125
  Great Basin Desert 136–137
  Great Victoria Desert 84–85
  Mojave Desert 40, 46–49
  Namib Desert 108–111
  Sahara Desert 36–37
  Thar Desert 60–61
polar deserts 15, 18, 140–153

R
rain shadow 18, 119, 131
rainfall 16, 18
reptiles 17, 33, 44–45, 56–57, 68–69, 80–83, 94, 121, 132
rock art 29
rock formations 23, 43, 118–119
Rub' al-Khali 74–75

S
sagebrush 128, 137
Sahara Desert 8, 18, 20, 28–37
salt flats 30, 66, 93
salt lakes 79, 92, 96
Sam Sand Dunes 52
sand 22–23
seals, southern elephant 142, 147
sediment 43
seif dunes 22
Serpentine Lakes 76
Sesriem Canyon 103
shipwrecks 112–113
sidewinders 17, 44–45
Simpson Desert 21
Skeleton Coast 112–113
Sonoran Desert 5, 20
Sossusvlei 105
South America 6–7
space 19
star dunes 22
storms 24, 38–39
succulents 17
Syrian Desert 21

T
Taklamakan Desert 11, 21
Tanami Desert 21
tectonic plates 130
temperatures 18, 19
terrain, tough 17
Thar Desert 52–63
thorny devils 82–83
toads, spadefoot 134–135
Trans-Altai Gobi 117
tree planting 25, 60
tumboa 110–11

INDEX

U, V
Uluru 13
Valley of the Moon 100–101
volcanoes 66, 118, 143

W, Y, Z
water
  erosion 22, 23
  finding/conserving 17, 32, 123
wildfires 129
wind erosion 22, 23, 31, 43
yardangs 23
yuccas 48–49

Acknowledgements

DK would like to thank the following people for their assistance in the preparation of this book: Soumya Rampal for editorial assistance; Ridhima Sikka and Samrajkumar S for picture research assistance; Helen Peters for the index; and Polly Goodman for proofreading.

The publisher would like to thank the following for their kind permission to reproduce their photographs:
(Key: a-above; b-below/bottom; c-centre; f-far; l-left; r-right; t-top)

1 Dreamstime.com: Jackreznor (Topography). **2–3 Dreamstime.com:** Jackreznor (Topography). **4–5 naturepl.com:** Jack Dykinga. **6–7 Greg Johnson. 8–9 Adobe Stock:** ImageBROKER / Thomas Dressler. **10–11 Getty Images:** Visual China Group / Wang Zhipeng. **12–13 Shutterstock.com:** Wirestock Creators. **14–15 Alamy Stock Photo:** Era-Images / Colin Harris. **16–19 Dreamstime.com:** Jackreznor (Topography). **17 Alamy Stock Photo:** ImageBROKER.com / Konrad Wothe (cra); Nature Picture Library / Solvin Zankl (crb). **naturepl.com:** Ugo Mellone (cr). **19 Alamy Stock Photo:** Claudio Caridi (t). **Getty Images:** Visual China Group (b). **22–23 Alamy Stock Photo:** Dorling Kindersley ltd (cb). **22–153 Dreamstime.com:** Jackreznor (Topography). **23 Adobe Stock:** Beata (tr). **Alamy Stock Photo:** Manfred Gottschalk (cra); Stefano Politi Markovina (tc); Michal Sikorski (ca). **24–25 Alamy Stock Photo:** Natural History Archive (tc). **24 Alamy Stock Photo:** Minden Pictures / Colin Monteath / Hedgehog House (b); Robertharding / Geoff Renner (crb). **Getty Images / iStock:** EcoPic (cl). **25 Getty Images / iStock:** Marcelo Silva (b). **26–27 Getty Images / iStock:** Asif Graphy. **28 Science Photo Library:** Mona Lisa Production / Thierry Berrod (tr). **29 Alamy Stock Photo:** Brother Luck (bc). **30–31 Getty Images / iStock:** Louis-Michel Desert (b). **31 Dreamstime.com:** Patrick Poendl (br). **Getty Images:** Stone / Philippe Lissac / Godong (ca). **32 Alamy Stock Photo:** Blickwinkel / Koenig (cr). **Dreamstime.com:** Matthijs Kuijpers (tl). **33 Adobe Stock:** Lauren (br). **Alamy Stock Photo:** Guillen Photo LLC / Amar and Isabelle Guillen (bl); Chris Mattison (tl);

ACKNOWLEDGEMENTS

Rosanne Tackaberry (cra). **34–35 Dreamstime.com:** Julian Schaldach. **34 Alamy Stock Photo:** Zoonar GmbH / Fotofeeling (bl). **35 Dreamstime.com:** Aleksandra Tokarz (ca). **Getty Images / iStock:** CharlesGibson (cr); Musat (bc). **36 Alamy Stock Photo:** GFC Collection (t). **37 Alamy Stock Photo:** Mauricio Abreu (cra). **Fabien Anthelme:** (tl). **Dreamstime.com:** Krystyna Wojciechowska Czarnik (cl); Abbas Rezzag (br). **38–39 Getty Images / iStock:** E+ / Pavliha. **41 Alamy Stock Photo:** Kip Evans (clb); Witold Skrypczak (br). **42–43 Adobe Stock:** Billy McDonald (c). **Dreamstime.com:** Maciej Bledowski (t). **43 Alamy Stock Photo:** AJFotos (bl). **44 Alamy Stock Photo:** imageBROKER.com / Mara Brandl (bl). **David R. Beaudette:** (tl). **44–45 Alamy Stock Photo:** Biosphoto / Daniel Heuclin (tc). **Minden Pictures:** Jurgen and Christine Sohns (bc). **45 Alamy Stock Photo:** Biosphoto / Daniel Heuclin (cra). **Depositphotos Inc:** YAYImages (clb). **46 Adobe Stock:** Diane N. Ennis (cr). **Alamy Stock Photo:** Gabbro (cla). **naturepl.com:** Steve Nicholls (bl). **46–47 Dreamstime.com:** Billy Mc Donald (t). **47 Alamy Stock Photo:** ImageBROKER.com / Michael Weber (br); Len Wilcox (cr). **48 Alamy Stock Photo:** Ron Niebrugge (clb). **48–49 naturepl.com:** Chris Mattison (c). **49 Alamy Stock Photo:** David Cobb (cb). **Dreamstime.com:** Darren Davis (cr); Jared Quentin (tc). **50–51 Alamy Stock Photo:** Andia / Joncheray. **52 Dreamstime.com:** Dmitry Rukhlenko (bc). **Getty Images / iStock:** Danielrao (cra). **54–55 Dreamstime.com:** Dmitry Rukhlenko. **55 Somnath Chatterjee:** (t). **56 Alamy Stock Photo:** Nature Picture Library / Bernard Castelein (tr); Hira Punjabi (crb). **Dreamstime.com:** Stu Porter (bl). **57 Alamy Stock Photo:** Travel4pictures (b). **Dreamstime.com:** Mihir Joshi (tr). **naturepl.com:** Laurent Geslin (cla). **58 Shutterstock.com:** Radheshyam Bishnoi (cla). **58–59 Getty Images / iStock:** ePhotocorp. **59 Ardea:** Joanna Van Gruisen / ardea.com (br). **60 Alamy Stock Photo:** Raquel Mogado (t). **Getty Images / iStock:** Ghulam Hussain (b). **60–61 Dreamstime.com:** Thana Ram (bc). **61 Dreamstime.com:** Deep Chand (tl). **Raghu Ghanapuram:** (br). **62–63 Alamy Stock Photo:** Jason Pemberton. **65 Adobe Stock:** ImageBROKER / Daniel Kreher (tr); Manu Nair (bl). **66 Alamy Stock Photo:** ImageBROKER / Fabian Von Poser (b). **Getty Images:** AFP (tl). **67 Alamy Stock Photo:** Westend61 GmbH. **68 Alamy Stock Photo:** Nature Picture Library / Xi Zhinong (cr). **Ardea:** Steve Downer / ardea.com (tc). **Shutterstock.com:** Cyrus Matiga (cla). **68–69 Alamy Stock Photo:** Eyal Bartov. **69 Alamy Stock Photo:** Blickwinkel / F. Teigler (crb); Andrew Gardner (tr). **naturepl.com:** David Shale (cla). **70 Alamy Stock Photo:** Holger Ehlers (tr). **Getty Images:** AFP / Karim Sahib (cla). **70–71 Alamy Stock Photo:** Nature Picture Library / Inaki Relanzon (c). **71 Alamy Stock Photo:** Nigel Cattlin (tr). **Shutterstock.com:** Osandi Yenulya (br). **72 Dreamstime.com:** Shakeelmsm (crb). **Getty Images / iStock:** Zanskar (bl). **Aklilu Negussie Mekuria:** (tl). **73 Alamy Stock Photo:** Biosphoto / Marie Aymerez (br). **Dreamstime.com:** Shakeelmsm (t). **naturepl.com:** Hanne & Jens Eriksen (clb). **74–75 Alamy Stock Photo:** ImageBROKER.com / Daniel Kreher. **76 Alamy Stock Photo:** Jason Edwards (tl). **Mark Chappell:** (bl). **78 Getty Images:** Photodisc / Ted Mead (bl). **Alan McCall:** (br). **78–79 Getty Images:** Stone / Ted Mead (t). **80 Avalon:** Ant (tr). **Dreamstime.com:** Ken Griffiths (b). **81 Alamy Stock Photo:** John Cancalosi (crb); Minden Pictures / D. Parer & E. Parer-Cook (cla). **Alinytjara Wilurara Landscape Board:** Brett Backhouse (bl). **82 Dreamstime.com:** Marc Witte (bl). **82–83 Alamy Stock Photo:** Natural Visions / Heather Angel. **83 Alamy Stock Photo:** Natural Visions / Heather Angel (br). **Dreamstime.com:** Robero Dani (tl). **84 Alamy Stock Photo:** Selfwood (b). **84–85 Alamy Stock Photo:** Mike Read (tc). **85 Alamy Stock Photo:** Nature Picture Library / Marie Lochman (bc). **Michael Brightwood:** (clb). **Dreamstime.com:** Aditya Riski Aziz (c). **Getty Images:** Universal Images Group / Auscape (tr). **86–87 Getty Images / iStock:** E+ / Philip Thurston. **88–89 Getty Images / iStock:** Erlantz Pérez Rodríguez. **91 Adobe Stock:** Freedom_Wanted (cra). **Alamy Stock Photo:** David Bebber (bl). **92 Shutterstock.com:** Aldo Olivera (b). **92–93 Dreamstime.com:** Nataliya Hora (t). **93 Dreamstime.com:** Albertoloyo (bc). **94 Alamy Stock Photo:** Premaphotos (cr). **Getty Images:** The Image Bank / Enrique Aguirre Aves (l). **naturepl.com:** Daniel Heuclin (b). **95 Alamy Stock Photo:** David Graham (tl). **naturepl.com:** Barrie Britton (clb). **96 Alamy Stock Photo:** Avalon.red / Photoshot (bl); Michael S. Nolan (tr); Philip Sharp (crb). **97 Getty Images / iStock:** Olga Tarasyuk. **98 Alamy Stock Photo:** Giulio Ercolani (cla). **98–99 Alamy Stock Photo:** Minden Pictures / Chris Stenger / Buiten-beeld (b). **Dreamstime.com:** Jeremy Richards (tc). **99 Alamy Stock Photo:** Minden Pictures / Sebastian Kennerknecht (tr). **Michail Belov:** (cl). **Kok van Herk:** (ca). **100–101 Dreamstime.com:** Positivetravelart. **103 Alamy Stock Photo:** Robertharding / Lee Frost (tr).

159

ACKNOWLEDGEMENTS

Dreamstime.com: Sergey Mayorov (bl). **104–105 Alamy Stock Photo:** Martin Harvey. **105 Alamy Stock Photo:** ImageBROKER.com / Christian Heinrich (tr). **naturepl.com:** Ernie Janes (br). **106–107 Alamy Stock Photo:** Minden Pictures / Theo Allofs (tc). **106 Alamy Stock Photo:** Image Professionals GmbH / Andreas Strauss (bl); Nature Picture Library / Emanuele Biggi (tl); Minden Pictures / Michael & Patricia Fogden (br). **107 Alamy Stock Photo:** Minden Pictures / Theo Allofs (b); Nature Picture Library / Solvin Zankl (tr). **108–109 Kok van Herk:** (tc). **naturepl.com:** Claudio Velasquez (bc). **108 Alamy Stock Photo:** Nature / Piemags (tl). **109 Alamy Stock Photo:** Nature / Piemags (cl). **Getty Images:** Stone / Paul Starosta (bc). **Shutterstock.com:** D. Kucharski K. Kucharska (r). **110 Alamy Stock Photo:** The Africa Image Library (cla). **110–111 Depositphotos Inc:** CezaryWojtkowski (b). **111 bihrmann.com:** (tc). **112–113 Alamy Stock Photo:** Gianni Marchetti. **114–115 Getty Images:** Moment / Guang Cao. **117 Alamy Stock Photo:** ImageBROKER / Bayar Balgantseren (bc); Nature Picture Library / Inaki Relanzon (crb). **118 Alamy Stock Photo:** Image Professionals GmbH / Jörg Reuther (cl). **118–119 Alamy Stock Photo:** Minden Pictures / Ingo Arndt (t). **119 Adobe Stock:** Danita Delimont (b). **120 Alamy Stock Photo:** AGAMI Photo Agency / James Eaton (c). **naturepl.com:** Klein & Hubert (tl). **120–121 Alamy Stock Photo:** ImageBROKER / Bernd Bieder (c). **121 Alamy Stock Photo:** Nilanjan Chatterjee (br); Glenn Welch (cla). **Jianong Li:** (tr). **122–123 Ardea:** ardea.com / M. Watson (c). **122 Dreamstime.com:** Vladislav Jirousek (clb). **123 Alamy Stock Photo:** Cordier Sylvain / Hemis.fr (br); Tom Radford (tr); Nature Picture Library / Valeriy Maleev (cla). **124 Bing Liu:** (l). **124–125 Adobe Stock:** Byyadnu (tc). **Dreamstime.com:** Homydesign (bc). **125 Adobe Stock:** LFRabanedo (tr). **Alamy Stock Photo:** Massimo Pizzotti (br). **Bayarmaa Chuluunbat:** (c). **126–127 Alamy Stock Photo:** Pavel Filatov. **128 Adobe Stock:** Anne Lindgren (tl). **Alamy Stock Photo:** James McLaughlin (bl). **130–131 Unsplash:** Aniket Deole (tc). **131 Dreamstime.com:** Elizabeth Cummings (c). **Shutterstock.com:** N Mrtgh (tr); Jacob Myslinski (br). **132 Alamy Stock Photo:** ImageBROKER.com / Marc Rasmus (crb). **Dreamstime.com:** Kcmatt (bl). **Getty Images / iStock:** Nattapong Assalee (cla). **133 Alamy Stock Photo:** Rick & Nora Bowers (cra); Brenda Tharp / DanitaDelimont (cla); Minden Pictures / Michael Durham (ca).

134–135 Alamy Stock Photo: All Canada Photos / Wayne Lynch (tc). Rye Jones. **134 Alamy Stock Photo:** John Sullivan (clb). **135 Alamy Stock Photo:** All Canada Photos / Wayne Lynch (br). **Brian Eagar:** (tr). **136 Alamy Stock Photo:** Piemags / Nature (tr, bl). **Getty Images / iStock:** Gerald Corsi (tl). **137 Adobe Stock:** Brendan (t). **Alamy Stock Photo:** Piemags / Nature (bl). **Depositphotos Inc:** Imagebrokermicrostock (br). **138–139 AWL Images:** Christian Heeb. **140–141 Dreamstime.com:** Staphy. **143 Alamy Stock Photo:** Blickwinkel / A. Rose (bc); Era-Images / Colin Harris (tr). **144 Alamy Stock Photo:** Robertharding / Michael Nolan (tr). **144–145 Getty Images:** Universal Images Group / Design Pics Editorial. **145 Dreamstime.com:** Staphy (tc). **146 Alamy Stock Photo:** Nature Picture Library / David Tipling (ca). **Science Photo Library:** British Antarctic Survey (tr). **147 Alamy Stock Photo:** Blickwinkel / Mcphoto / Pum (br); Chris Gomersall (clb). **Rémi Bigonneau:** (tl). **Getty Images:** Slowmotiongli (tr). **148–149 naturepl.com:** Frederique Olivier (tc). **Shutterstock.com:** Sergey 402. **149 Alamy Stock Photo:** Nature Picture Library / Fred Olivier (br). **150 Shutterstock.com:** Best-Backgrounds (cl). **150–151 Alamy Stock Photo:** David Lazenby (b). **Science Photo Library:** Arcady Zakharov (tc). **151 Alamy Stock Photo:** Piemags / Nature (cra). **152–153 Dreamstime.com:** Jonathan Green

Cover images: *Front and Back:* **Adobe Stock:** Brendan cb; **Dreamstime.com:** Antonprado b, Fotosutra t; *Front:* **Alamy Stock Photo:** Piemags / Nature br, Outback Australia ca; **Dreamstime.com:** Vitaly Korovin bl; **Getty Images / iStock:** Zanskar clb; *Back:* **Alamy Stock Photo:** Piemags / Nature bl, Outback Australia ca; **Getty Images / iStock:** Zanskar clb